MARRIAGE BONDS
and
MINISTERS' RETURNS
of
PITTSYLVANIA COUNTY, VIRGINIA
1767–1805

COMPILED AND PUBLISHED
by
CATHERINE LINDSAY KNORR
1956

Please Direct All Correspondence and Book Orders to:

**Southern Historical Press, Inc.
P.O. Box 1267
375 West Broad Street
Greenville, S.C. 29602-1267**

ISBN # 0-89308-260-0

Printed in the United States of America

To
Mrs. Philip Wallace Hiden
(Martha Woodroof)
to whom has been trusted Virginia's
priceless records and to whom the
genealogists and historians all
over America, and especially Virginia, owe an immeasurable debt of
gratitude for her work in having
those records restored and safe
guarded.

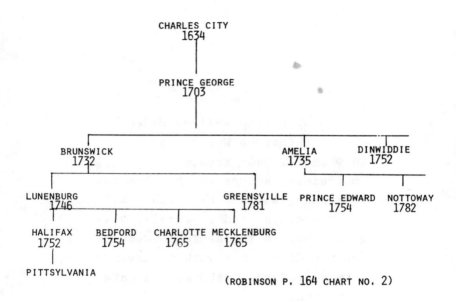

CHARLES CITY
1634

PRINCE GEORGE
1703

BRUNSWICK
1732

AMELIA
1735

DINWIDDIE
1752

LUNENBURG
1746

GREENSVILLE
1781

PRINCE EDWARD
1754

NOTTOWAY
1782

HALIFAX
1752

BEDFORD
1754

CHARLOTTE
1765

MECKLENBURG
1765

PITTSYLVANIA

(ROBINSON P. 164 CHART NO. 2)

Bedford   Campbell   Charlotte

Franklin   Chatham ⊙

Henry   PITTSYLVANIA   Halifax   Mecklenburg

Preface

When Virginia named Pittsylvania County for William Pitt, Earl of Chatham, the celebrated English statesman and great friend of the American Colonies she really went all out to honor the man who took such a prominent part in securing repeal of the odious Stamp Act of 1766 because she also named the county seat Chatham (Robinson 188).

Pittsylvania was formed 1767 from Halifax which had been formed 1752 from Lunenburg which had come out of Brunswick in 1745. At that time Pittsylvania embraced the present Patrick and Henry both formed in 1777. The County has been its present size since that date.

Pittsylvania Order Book I states that the first Court was held on Friday 26 June 1767. Justices present were: Thomas Dillard, Archibald Gordon, Hugh Innes, James Roberts, John Donelson, Theophelus Lacy, John Wilson, Peter Copland, John Hanly, Harmon Critz, John Dix, Peter Perkins, George Jefferson and Benjamin Lankford.

William Tunstall was first County Clerk; first Sheriff, Benjamin Lankford, his deputies Abram Shelton and William Ward.

Producing licenses to practise as a-torneys-at-law were Isaac Read, Edmund Winston and John Williams, Gentlemen.

The first County Lieutenant was John Donelson (McAllister pp 100-101) who lived at "Markham" on Banister River 12 miles east of Chatham. He became one of the founders of Tennessee and father of Rachel who married Andrew Jackson seventh President of the United States.

The first Burgesses to represent the new County of Pittsylvania in the House of Burgesses, Assembly of 17 May 1769, were John Donelson and Hugh Innes.

The old Book of Surveys in the court house shows an interesting plat of the first survey of the present town of Chatham in 1807 then called Competition because of the inability of the Pittsylvanians to decide on the location of the County Seat.

There were 8 acres laid off in half acre lots by Joshua Stone, surveyor. His fee was $12.00. The trustees of the town to vote this expenditure were: Daniel Coleman, John Dabney, Thomas M. Clark, William Tunstall, Joseph Lankford, Francis Dabney, Joseph Carter and William Young. Col. Daniel Coleman was appointed President and it was ordered that Francis Dabney be appointed Clerk of the Board.

James F. Johnston bought lots 1, 2 and 3; the rest of the lots were sold as follows: Godfrey Burnett nos. 4 and 10; John Hall no. 5; William Clark nos. 6 and 8; William Rawlins no. 7; George M. Watson no. 9; Francis Dabney no. 11; and Josiah Ferguson, Jr., no. 12.

Plat

4	5	12
3	6	11
2	7	10
1	8	9

One thing that puzzled me about the Pittsylvania records
was the duplicate marriages. Obviously the same couple,
there would be several years difference between the bonds and
the ministers' returns. And "curiouser and curiouser" as Alice
in Wonderland says, the ministers' return often ante dated
the bond. And that just can't be. Where there was a modicum
of doubt as to there being two couples I have let both stand.
The following are samples: John Kendrick married Ann Neal
in 1780 and in 1782; Thomas Bleakley married Rebecca Ward in
1796 and again in 1800; William Dodson married Tabitha
Hendrick in 1794 and in 1796; Richard White married Peggy
Donald in 1767 and Margaret Donald in 1768. The last are two
different bonds with two different sureties. Henry Perkins
married Bethinia Cabell in 1796 and Bethaina Cahall in 1802;
Martin Wilson married both Rhoda Wilson and Rhoda Stamps in
1800. There two entries for every above cited marriage in
the Pittsylvania Marriage Register. I could and did check
the date of the bond by the original bond but I found no
original list of ministers' returns by which to check the
register.

One piece of luck befell me in Chatham. I met Mrs.
Randolph V. Overbey in the Court House. She is not an employee
so it was pure chance that brought her to me. She calls her-
self an amateur genealogist but the way she operates I'd
designate her as professional and one of the best at that.
She worked right with me copying things I'd find or finding
things for me to copy. Nobody knows what it meant to me to
have her very efficient help. Should any one need assistance
in Pittsylvania her address is Box 53, Chatham, Virginia.

In the Court House is a record of the formation of
Camden Parish of the Episcopal Church. This was one of the
priceless things Hensen Overbey brought to my attention.

Camden Parish, Pittsylvania County was formed the same
year as the County, the first meeting of the Vestry being held
21 June 1767. The following were vestrymen present: John
Donaldson, John Pigg, Hugh Innes, George Rowland, Cripsin
Shelton, John Willson, Peter Perkins, Abraham Shelton,
Theophilus Lacy, Robert Chandler and William Witcher. Benjamin
Lankford was appointed Clerk of the Vestry and George Rowland
and Abraham Shelton were appointed Church Wardens. Lewis
Morgan was Reader of the new Parish. He was to "read at the
Chappell at Snow Creek, Potter's Creek and at the house of
William Heard."

The first Rector seems to have been Rev. Alexander Gordon who "came unto the Vestry and agrees for 1000 pounds of tobacco to preach at Abraham Shelton's, at the Meeting House at Potter's Creek, at Snow Creek Chappell, at John Vanbebber's, Peter Copeland's, Haman Crites' and Edward Smith's".

The Chatham Chamber of Commerce publishes a little brochurs setting forth the advantages of living in such a sweet, shady, quiet place. From it I learned that modern Pittsylvania County has an annual tobacco crop of twenty million dollars. So tobacco is still a legal tender just as it was in Rev. Gordon's day. And there must be something more to Chatham than shade and quiet. The folder doesn't say a word about the courtesy of the people. I parked my car, marched in the bank and asked where was the County Clerk's office. A gentleman took me clear out on the side walk and pointed out the Court House next door that I had passed in my preoccupation with finding a place to park on the busy main street. And look at the way Hensen Overbey pitched in to help me the very first time she ever laid eyes on me!

The Chamber of Commerce is right when it says: "Chatham: a wonderful place to taise a family." If I had another family to raise I'd be right there.

                                    Catherine Lindsay Knorr

Mrs. H.A. Knorr

29 August 1795. Abraham AARON, Jr., and Chloe Pearson. Sur. John Pearson. p. 20

7 February 1797. Isaac AARON and Polley Walker, dau. of Elisha Walker who consents. Sur. Jacob Arnn. p. 23

15 February 1790. Francis ABSTON and Salley Farmer, dau. of Thomas Farmer who consents. Sur. John W. Clements. Married by Rev. James Kinney. p. 12

29 July 1789. John ABSTON and Frances Thurman, dau. of Zithard Thurman who consents. Sur. William Clements. Married by Rev. Richard Elliott. p. 11

15 April 1785. Elijah ADAMS and Elizabeth Maneas. Married by Rev. Samuel Harris. p. 7

21 November 1780. George ADAMS and Esebell Wilson. Sur. Sylvester Adams. p. 3

--- --- 1795. Harris ADAMS and Frances Chattin. Married by Rev. Matthew Bates. p. 20

--- --- 1800. Joel ADAMS and Dionisha Walden. Married by Rev. John Jenkins. p. 28

22 December 1804. Joel ADAMS and Janey Payne. Sur. Dudley Farthing. Married by Rev. Thomas Payne. p. 36

9 February 1796. John ADAMS and Nancy Burton, dau. of Elijah Burton who consents. Sur. Thomas Prosize. p. 22

21 December 1803. John ADAMS and Martha Walken, dau. of Charles Walden who consents and is surety. p. 34

14 January 1803. Joshua ADAMS and Tabitha Brooks. Sur. Gabriel Brooks. Signs her own consent. p. 34

8 March 1797. Larkin ADAMS and Nancy Chambers. Sur. Martin Hardin. Married by Rev. Richard Elliott. p. 23

15 November 1804. Lewis ADAMS and Molley Meade, dau. of James Meade who consents. Sur. William Williams. Married by Rev. David Nowlin. p. 36

19 July 1790. Nathan ADAMS and Agness Campbell, dau. of Abram Campbell who consents. Sur. George Watson. Married by Rev. Richard Elliott. p. 12

8 March 1787. Simon ADAMS and Henrietta Dix. Married by Rev.
Samuel Harris. p. 9

10 February 1796. Spencer ADAMS and Sarah Corbin, dau. of
Rawley Corbin who consents. Sur. Charles Womack. p. 22

15 August 1795. William ADAMS and Fanney Meachum, dau. of More
Meachum who consents. Sur. John Wright. Married by Rev.
Richard Elliott, who says Fanny Mitcham. p. 20

7 October 1799. Henry ADKERSON and Elizabeth Rossett, dau. of
Sam Rossett who consents. Sur. William Reynolds. p. 26

16 March 1792. Abner ADKINS and Barbery Crust. Sur. Samuel
Read. p. 15

5 May 1805. Drury ADKINS and Susanna Price, dau. of William
Price, Sr. who consents. Sur. John Price. p. 38

19 December 1796. John ADKINS and Salley Owen. Sur. William
Owen. Married by Rev. James Tompkins. p. 22

12 February 1799. Lewis ADKINS and Susannah Keezee. Sur.
John Keezee. p. 26

9 December 1805. William ADKINS and Betsy Thacker. Sur.
Joseph Thacker. Married by Rev. Willis Hopwood. p. 38

14 December 1798. Winston ADKINS and Molley Allen Thacker.
Sur. Reubin Thacker. Married by Rev. James Tompkins. p. 25

13 February 1786. Elisha AIRES and Lidia Owen. Married by
Rev. Lazarus Dodson. p. 8

16 March 1802. Achilles ALLEN and Polley Royall. Sur. Robert
Ferguson. p. 32

16 December 1780. James ALLEN and Nany Dyer. Sur. Elijah
Dyer. p. 3

25 August 1785. James ALLEN and Cloey Vaughan. Sur. John
Vaughan. Shouldn't this be Chloe? p. 7

20 January 1794. James ALLEN and Anne Collier, dau. of John
Collier who consents. Sur. Ambrose Collier. Married by Rev.
James Kinney. p. 18

2 March 1796. Thomas ALLSUP and Alice Williams. Sur. John
Spurlin. p. 22

24 December 1792. Francis ANDERSON and Salley Mottley, dau.
of Joseph Mottley who consents. Sur. Elkanah Echols. Married
by Rev. Matthew Bates. p. 15

13 November 1797. John ANDERSON and Sally Callaway, dau. of Charles Callaway who consents. Sur. Achilles Callaway. p. 23

16 January 1783. Matthew ANDERSON and Martha Tanner. Married by Rev. Lazarus Dodson. p. 5

15 December 1794. Eben ANGEL and Elizabeth Doss, dau. of James Doss who consents. Sur. Charles Wright. Married by Rev. James Kinney. p. 18

18 November 1793. Henry ARNOLD and Nancy Davis, dau. of Thomas Davis who consents. p. 17

9 October 1801. Thomas ARNOLD and Nancy Terry, dau. of James Terry who consents. Sur. Obediah Echols. Married by Rev. Richard Elliott. p. 31

20 December 1802. Isaac ARON and Elizabeth Fuller, dau. of Zachariah Fuller who consents. Sur. Joseph Fuller. p. 32

20 December 1790. Jacob ARON and Judith Kearby (Kirby), consent of John Bartee stepfather of Judith, and of Dicy Bartee, her mother. Sur. George Thurman. John Bartee married Dicey Kirby 4 Sept. 1786 in Franklin Co. p. 12

20 September 1802. Abraham ARNN, Jr., and Nelly Perdue. Sur. George Arnn. Signs her own consent. p. 32

10 December 1797. George ARNN and Sarah Walker, dau. of Elisha and Judy Walker who consent. Sur. John Walker. Shouldn't this be Aaron? p. 23

18 September 1782. Moses ARN and Abigail Payne. Married by Rev. Lazarus Dodson. p. 3

--- --- 1800. Barnaby ARTHUR and Mary Bardick. Married by Rev. Thomas Douglas. p. 28

23 May 1782. James ARTHUR and Nancy Bennett. Married by Rev. John Bailey. p. 3

30 December 1793. Stephen ARTHUR and Jane Morton, dau. of John Morton, Sr., who consents. Sur. Gilbert Dear. p. 17

22 March 1802. Joel ASHER and Polley Ramsey, dau. of Cloe Ramsey who consents. Sur. Richard Ramsey. p. 32

30 December 1802. Sterling ASHER and Betsey Tomblin. Sur. Joseph Tomblin. p. 32

6 September 1785. Jesse ASHLOCK and Anne Scott. Sur. Joseph Hill. Married by Rev. Samuel Harris. p. 7

7 November 1785. William ASHLOCK and Sarah Sullians. Married by Rev. Lazarus Dodson. p. 7

26 March 1779. William ASTIN and Margaret Wilson. Sur. Joseph Akin. Signs her own consent. p. 2

--- --- 1800. Joel ATKINS and Sarah Standley. Married by Rev. Thomas Douglas. p. 28

26 October 1786. John ATKINS and Winney Dyer. Married by Rev. David Barr. p. 8

15 June 1801. Lewis ATKINS and Sally Taylor. Sur. James Taylor. Married by Rev. Thomas Payne. p. 31

15 April 1805. Jesse ATKINSON and Rachel Madding, dau. of Salley Madding who consents. Sur. Samuel Atkinson. Married by Rev. John Atkinson. p. 38

9 April 1780. Joel ATKINSON and Rachel Emmerson, dau. of Samuel Emmerson who consents. Sur. Joseph Akin. p. 3

27 July 1796. Champness AUSTIN and Aincy Dear. Sur. William Austin. p. 22

8 January 1797. David AUSTIN and Elizabeth Oliver. Sur. William Austin. p. 23

26 November 1777. Joseph AUSTIN and Wealthy Prewet. Sur. William Goggin. Signs her own consent. p. 2

23 April 1800. Stephen AUSTIN and Rebecca Hankins. Sur. Reubin Hankins. Signs her own consent. Married by Rev. Clement Nance. p. 28

20 November 1797. William BABER and Nancy Patterson. Sur. Nathan Thurman. Signs her own consent. p. 23

16 September 1805. John BAILESS and Lena Compton. Sur. Nehemiah Compton. p. 38

16 September 1796. Charles BAILEY and Mary Allen. Married by Rev. Richard Elliott. p. 22

17 December 1804. Christopher BAILEY and Winifred Dove, dau. of William Dove who consents. Sur. Leonard Dove. Married by Rev. Griffith Dickinson. p. 36

23 April 1797. Peter James BAILEY and Ellenor Short. Married by Rev. Richard Elliott. p. 23

8 March 1791. Thomas BALL and Elender Dyer, dau. of James Dyer who consents. Sur. Alexander Mahan. Married by Rev. James Hurt. p. 14

---- March 1789. John BALLINGER and Lithe Lester. p. 11

22 December 1802. Allen BARBER and Isbell McDaniel, dau. of Sally McDaniel who consents. Sur. William Barker. p. 32

15 July 1794. Elisha Dyer BARBER and Drusilla Thurman, dau. of Nathan Thurman who consents. Sur. Hez. Barber. Married by Rev. James Kinney. p. 18

18 January 1793. Hezekiah BARBER and Elizabeth Smith. William Smith consents for Elizabeth. Sur. Samuel Dalton. Married by Rev. Matthew Bates. p. 17

7 February 1789. Joseph BARBER and Jean Goad, dau. of Charles Goad who consents. Sur. Thomas Dalton. Married by Rev. James Kinney. p. 11

19 January 1795. Joseph BARBER and Nancy Goad, dau. of Charles Goad who consents. Sur. Samuel Dalton. Married by Rev. Joseph Drury. p. 20

20 March 1801. Stephen BARBER and Patsey Reynolds, dau. of Jesse Reynolds who consents. Sur. John Hubbard. Married by Rev. Richard Elliott. p. 31

11 August 1785. William BARBER and Nancy Turley. Married by Rev. David Barr. p. 7

23 December 1799. John BARGER and Peggy Hedrick. Married by Rev. Thomas Payne. p. 26

17 December 1782. Benjamin BARGIS and Virlinda Simson. Married by Rev. Lazarus Dodson. p. 4

9 September 1794. Jeremiah BARKER and Anne Mustain. Married by Rev. Thomas Payne. p. 18

9 February 1782. Jesse BARKER and Mary Barker. Married by Rev. John Bailey. p. 3

--- --- 1803. Joseph BARKER and Isabel McDaniel. Married by Rev. Thomas Sparks. p. 34

5 January 1804. Joseph BARKER and Salley McDaniel. Sur. Clement McDaniel. Nancy McDaniel consents for Salley. p. 36

4 April 1792. Moses BARKER and Nancy Harris. Sur. John Hardwick, Jr. Married by Rev. Richard Elliott. p. 15

2 August 1782. Henry H. BARKSDALE and Molley Bayne, dau. of Richard Bayne who consents. Sur. J.M. Williams. p. 3

26 April 1802. Jesse BARLOW and Nancy Gosnell. Sur. Joseph Gosnell. Married by Rev. Clement Nance. p. 32

22 October 1792. William BARNES and Sarah Connor. Sur. Jesse Barnes. Consent of Peyton and Elizabeth Hampton "father and mother". Shouldn't this be step-father and of which one? p. 15

20 June 1803. John BARNETT and Susanna Sutherlin, dau. of Thomas Sutherlin who consents. Sur. James Gatewood. p. 34

--- --- 1790. John BARROTT and Ellenor Robbin. Married by Rev. John Jenkins. p. 12

--- --- 1804. Joseph BASS and Ann J. Dawson. Married by Rev. John Jenkins. p. 36

22 January 1782. William BASS and Paty Mullings. Married by Rev. James Robinson. Shouldn't this be Patty Mullins? p. 4

17 August 1782. Robert BATEMAN and Betsy Harness. Married by Rev. John Bailey. p. 4

20 December 1791. William BATEMAN and Elizabeth Thomas. Sur. David Tompkins. p. 14

25 April 1788. James BATES and Susanna Witt. Married by Rev. Lazarus Dodson. p. 10

30 December 1788. Matthew BATES and Mary B. Jones. Floyd Tanner guardian of Mary, consents. Sur. George Robinson. Married by James Hinton. p. 10

--- --- 1793. Samuel BATES and Martha Astin. Married by Rev. Matthew Bates. p. 17

27 September 1794. John BAYES and Sally Owen, dau. of Richard Owen who consents. Sur. Thomas Ham. Married by Rev. Matthew Bates. p. 18

--- --- 1799. Joshua BAYS and Ruth Saunders. Married by Rev. John Jenkins. p. 26

14 March 1786. Rice BEADLES and Salley Adams, dau. of Nathaniel Adams who consents. Sur. Benjamin Davis. Married by Rev. Samuel Harris. p. 8

6 June 1789. Seaton BEADLES and Sarah Pendleton. Sur. Jesse Law. Signs her own consent. p. 11

1 April 1786. Shadrack BEAL and --- ----. Sur. Joel Short.
p. 7

26 November 1782. John BEALE and Rebecca Bayes. Sur. James
George. Signs her own consent. p. 3

8 February 1790. Richard BEASLEY and Susanna Terry. Sur.
Thomas Terry. Married by Rev. James Kinney. Married by Rev.
Thomas Douglas. p. 12

8 February 1790. William BEAVERS and Nancy McDaniel, dau. of
Ann McDaniel who consents. Sur. Daniel Price. Married by
Rev. William Heath. p. 12

1 March 1802. William BEAVERS and Elizabeth Fontaine, dau.
of Moese and Elizabeth Fontaine who consent. Sur. Peter
Fontaine. p. 32

--- --- 1800. George BECK and Amey Dyer. Married by Rev.
Thomas Douglas. p. 28

11 February 1793. James BECK and Rosannah Dodson, dau. of
William Dodson who consents. Sur. John Burnett. p. 17

21 November 1797. William BECK and Nancy Boaz, dau. of Agness
Boaz who consents. Sur. Daniel Boaz. p. 23

19 January 1792. Samuel BEENS and Rachel Pigg, sister of
Peter Pigg, who consents. Sur. James Gammon. p. 15

29 August 1792. Leonard BELL and Stony Ferguson. Sur. Daniel
Wersham. p. 15

7 January 1786. Elijah BENNETT and Martha Sutton. Sur. James
Bennet. Married by Rev. David Barr. p. 8

3 August 1793. Hezekiah BENNETT and Frances Hardy, dau. of
Benjamin Hardy who consents. Sur. Jesse Hardy. Married by
Rev. Lazarus Dodson. p. 17

6 March 1795. John BENNETT and Polley Lewis, dau. of Mary
Ann Lewis who consents. Sur. Hezekiah Bennett. Married by
Rev. Lazarus Dodson. p. 20

7 November 1796. John BENNETT and Polley Terry. Sur. Benjamin
Terry. Married by Rev. Lazarus Dodson. p. 22

8 August 1805. John BENNETT and Nancy Waddill, dau. of William
Waddill who consents. Sur. Thomas Vaughan. p. 38

20 August 1799. Micajah Wheeler BENNETT and Patsey Pullen,
dau. of Thomas Pullen who consents. Married by Rev. John
Jenkins. p. 26

29 December 1803. Peter BENNETT and Mourning Bobbett. Sur.
Charles Bobbett. Married by Rev. David Nowlin. p. 34

12 May 1787. Richard BENNETT and Elizabeth Ferguson. Sur. Robert Williams. Married by Rev. Lazarus Dodson. p. 9

21 November 1795. Richard BENNETT and Asenna Dalton. Sur. John Dalton. Married by Rev. James Kinney. p. 20

18 November 1799. Richard BENNETT and Nancy Dalton, dau. of John Dalton who consents. Sur. Charles Bobbitt. Married by Rev. Thomas Payne. p. 26

20 December 1790. Stephen BENNETT and Lucy Nowlin. Bryant W. Nowlin consents for Lucy. Sur. Peyton Nowlin. p. 12

29 May 1798. Travis BENNETT and Jenney Going. Sur. John Bennett. Lilly Logan signs certificate. p. 25

27 January 1800. Jacob BERGER and Catey Nowlin. Bryant W. Nowlin consents for Catey. Sur. David Nowlin. p. 28

23 November 1799. David BERRY and Sarah Cunningham, dau. of Nathan Cunningham who consents. Sur. Jeremiah Cole. John Berry father of David. p. 26

11 January 1795. Robert BIGGERS and Bettsey W. Matthews. Sur. William Devin. Married by Rev. Richard Elliott. p. 20

8 October 1804. William BIGGERS and Polley V. Thomas, dau. of Henry and Margaret Rawlings who consent. Sur. James Devin. Married by Rev. Richard Elliott. Henry Rawlings was Polley's stepfather having married her mother, Margaret Thomas 21 Nov. 1795. p. 36

8 January 1795. Edmond BINGHAM and Lucy Bayes, dau. of John Bayes who consents. Sur. Joseph Mayes. p. 20

10 July 1787. James BLACKBURN and Febe (Phoebe) Burton. Married by Rev. Samuel Harris. p. 9

18 April 1796. George BLAIR and Martha Fulton. Sur. George Hankins. p. 22

1 April 1796. James BLAIR and Polley Dickinson, dau. of Frances Dickinson who consents. Sur. George Blair. p. 22

18 May 1801. William BLAIR and Nancy Thomas, dau. of Benjamin Thomas who consents. Sur. William Thomas. p. 31

19 March 1794. Thomas BLAKE and Abagial Slone (Abigail?). Married by Rev. Lazarus Dodson. p. 18

18 January 1797. Charles BLAKELEY and Sally Turtle. Sur. Joshua Saffel. p. 23

2 August 1783. John BLAKELY and Jean Shields, dau. of Samuel
Shields who consents. Sur. Joseph Akin. p. 5

9 January 1795. John BLANKS and Nancy Epperson, dau. of William
Epperson who consents. Sur. William Farthing. p. 20

8 March 1795. Joseph BLANKS and Frankey James. Sur. William
Farthing. Signs her own consent. p. 20

12 January 1791. James BLEAKLEY and Elizabeth Smith. Sur.
Robert Devin. Signs her own consent. Married by Rev. Richard
Elliott. p. 14

6 December 1796. Thomas BLEAKELY and Rebecca Ward. Sur.
David Frizzell. p. 22

-- --- 1800. Thomas BLEAKLEY and Rebeckah Ward. Married by
Rev. Thomas Douglas. p. 28

12 November 1770. Dillion BLEVINS and Ann Armstrong. John
Rowland signs the certificate. p. 1

3 October 1796. Edmund BOAZ and Salley Thurman, dau. of John
and Nancy Thurman who consent. Sur. William Thurman. Married
by Rev. James Tompkins. p. 22

16 January 1796. Daniel BOAZ and Lydia Inman, dau. of William
and Susanna Inman who consent. Sur. Richard Beck. Married by
Rev. James Tompkins. p. 22

2 February 1788. Henry BOAZ and Polley Hester, dau. of Charles
Hester who consents. Sur. Armistead Dudley. p. 10

27 August 1804. Thomas BOAZ and Lucy Davis. Married by Rev.
William White. p. 36

29 August 1796. Alexander BOHANNON and Mary Hill. Sur. Joseph
Hill who consents for Mary. Married by Rev. John Atkinson. p. 22

17 March 1788. Jarrett BOLLING and Nancy Watts. Sur. Richard
Watts. p. 10

1 October 1785. James BOLTON and Fanny Clarkson. Married by
Rev. David Barr. p. 7

10 February 1785. John BOLTON and Christian Wynne. Married
by Rev. Samuel Harris. p. 7

12 November 1785. Robert BOLTON and Salley Russell. Married
by Rev. David Barr. p. 7

14 January 1787. Thomas BOLTON and Phebe Waller. Sur. John
Waller. Married by Rev. Samuel Harris. p. 9

16 October 1797. Joseph BONDURANT and Rhoda Terry. Sur. John
Terry. Signs her own consent. Married by Rev. John Jenkins.
p. 23

19 January 1795. Charles BOOTH and Mary Barber. Sur. Matthews
Sparks. Signs her own consent. p. 20

6 June 1801. Eppa BOOTH and Amy Tucker. Sur. Lewis Tucker.
p. 31

16 June 1799. Morris BOOTH and Susanna Billings. Sur. Richard
Ramsey. p. 26

10 January 1782. William BOSKETT and Ann Gooch. Married by
Rev. James Robinson. p. 3

21 June 1790. Jesse BOW and Rhodey Thurman. Sur. Richard
Thurman. Married by Rev. James Kinney. p. 12

8 November 1792. William BOYED and Frances Cook. Married by
Rev. Lazarus Dodson. p. 15

23 May 1782. John BOZWELL and Mary Conway. Married by Rev.
John Bailey. p. 4

12 January 1793. Charles BOZZELL and Nancy Keezee. John
Keezee consents for Nancy. Sur. Barney Bozzell. Married by
Rev. Thomas Douglas. p. 17

17 May 1784. Daniel BRADLEY and Elizabeth Davis. Sur. Benjamin
Davis. Married by Rev. John Bailey. p. 5

29 May 1797. John BRADLEY and Oney Parrott. Sur. Laban
Thurman. Signs her own consent. Married by Rev. James Kinney.
p. 23

15 August 1785. William BRADLEY and Salley Prosize. Sur.
George Prosize. Signs her own consent. Married by Rev.
David Barr. p. 7

19 October 1790. Michael BRANSOM and Mary Hammock, dau. of
Richard and Mary Hammock who consent. Sur. Hezekiah Bransom.
p. 12

7 May 1803. Henry BRANSON and Elizabeth Lewis. Sur. Briscoe
Branson. p. 34

17 February 1800. John BRANSON and Jane Norton, dau. of John
Norton who consents. Sur. Henry W. Norton. p. 28

30 November 1786. Benjamin BRAWNER and Mary Rogers. Sur. Isham
Farmer. Married by Rev. Lazarus Dodson. p. 8

25 November 1768. Ambrose BREMLETT and Jean Woodson. Sur. Adam
Loving. Wit. John Burch, stepfather and Charity Burch mother.
John Burch m. Charity Woodson, widow, 28 Aug. 1756 in Cumberland
Co. p. 1

18 February 1788. James BRENT and Ann Patrick, dau. of John Patrick who consents. Sur. James George. p. 10

21 July 1779. Caleb BREWER and Polley Hundley. Sur. James Brewer. p. 2

12 August 1782. John BREWER and Pattsey Brewer. Sur. James Brewer. p. 3

14 February 1785. Sackville BREWER and Fanny Hopkins. Sur. Joseph Akin. Sam Calland signs certificate. Married by Rev. David Barr. p. 7

8 January 1784. William BRIDGWATERS and Susannah Burges. Married by Rev. John Bailey. p. 5

13 November 1795. George BROCK and Amey Dyer. Sur. William Dyer. Signs her own consent. p. 20

24 December 1798. John T. BROCK and Frances Shackleford (widow). Sur. Henry T. Wright. Signs her own consent. Married by Rev. William Wright. p. 25

20 July 1795. William BROCK and Phebe Blackburn. Sur. Benjamin Burton. Signs her own consent. James and Sarah Burton sign the certificate. p. 20

4 January 1803. Samuel BROOKS and Polley Roberts (Bingham). Sur. John Roberts alias Bingham. Signs her own consent as Polley Roberts alias Bingham. Married by Rev. Griffith Dickinson. p. 34

29 July 1803. Gabriel BROOKS and Nancy Arnold. Sur. Joshua Adams. Signs her own consent. p. 34

2 December 1782. Isham BROWDEN and Frances Daniel. Sur. --- Wilson. Signs her own consent. p. 3

28 September 1803. Frederick BROWN and Nancy Reynolds, dau. of Jesse Reanonds who consents. Sur. Lemuel Matherley. Married by Rev. James Nelson. p. 34

2 March 1785. James BROWN and Hannah Abbott. Married by Rev. Samuel Harris. p. 7

11 April 1799. John BROWN and Mary Hoyle, dau. of Charles Hoyle who consents. Sur. Walter Lamp. p. 26

4 March 1784. Samuel BROWN and Pheby Clarke. Married by Rev. Thomas Sparks. p. 5

11 January 1786. Alexander BRUCE and Frances Hall. Sur. John Hall. Married by Rev. Samuel Harris. p. 8

-- --- 1794. John BRUCE and Lucy Doss. Married by Rev. Matthew Bates. p. 18

15 February 1786. James BRUMMET and Sarah Reice, dau. of John Reice who consents. Sur. Allen Brock. Married by Rev. David Barr. p. 8

19 November 1787. John BRUMMET and Prudence McKenney. Sur. William Evans. p. 9

3 October 1805. Elisha BRYANT and Edith Douglas. Sur. Nehemiah Kelley. p. 38

16 December 1805. Nelson BRYANT and Elizabeth Petty. Sur. Thomas Elliott. p. 38

12 January 1797. William BRYANT and Elizabeth Murray. Married by Rev. George Dodson. p. 23

27 July 1804. Severn BUCEY and Polley Ferguson. Sur. Leonard Beall. Married by Rev. Richard Elliott. p. 36

18 April 1805. Jesse BUCKLEY and Elizabeth Keatts. Married by Rev. Griffith Dickinson. p. 38

24 October 1786. John BUCKLEY and Polley Harris. Married by Rev. Lazarus Dodson. p. 8

6 September 1784. Thomas BUCKNALL and Nancy Deropit. Married by Rev. David Barr. p. 5

17 April 1797. John BULLINGTON and Cluree Mitchell. Sur. William Mitchell. p. 23

5 December 1793. William BULLINGTON and Jane Harris, dau. of David Harris who consents. Sur. William Harris. p. 17

24 May 1802. Reubin BURDEN and Sally Chany. Sur. Ezekial Chany. Joseph Chaney consents for Sally. p. 32

19 December 1785. Elias BURGESS and Sarah Burgess. Sur. Tech Prenet. p. 7

12 August 1799. John BURGESS and Polley McMillian, dau. of Nancy Muckmillian who consents. Sur. James Watkins. Married by Rev. Clement Nance. p. 26

29 December 1789. Benjamin BURNETT and Mary Dunn. Sur. John Dunn. Married by Rev. Richard Elliott. p. 11

-- --- 1793. Edward BURNETT and Dolley -----. Sur. Godfrey Brunett. p. 17

5 October 1780. Henry BURNETT and Eliza Shields. Sur. Joshua Cantrell. Signs her own consent. This should be Elizabeth. p.3

21 June 1785. James BURNETT and Margaret Robinson. Married by Rev. David Barr. p. 7

7 January 1799. James C. BURNETT and Keziah Pulliam, dau. of Drury Pulliam who consents. Sur. William Pulliam. p. 26

3 January 1798. Jeremiah BURNETT and Sarah Bird. Sur. James Tompkins. Signs her own consent. p. 25

24 December 1791. John BURNETT and Linda Harvey. Sur. Edward Burnett. Married by Rev. Richard Elliott. p. 14

13 March 1792. John BURNETT and Judith Becke. Sur. James Burnett. Signs her own consent. p. 15

22 January 1800. Thomas BURNETT and Elizabeth Shaw. Sur. Jeremiah Burnett. Signs her own consent. p. 28

19 December 1801. Isham BURTON and Annice Dyer. Sur. Harmon Dyer. p. 31

19 December 1803. John BURTON and Edah. Allen. Sur. James Allen. p. 34

4 August 1794. Joseph BURTON and Dorothy Nance, dau. of Clement and Mary Nance who consent. Sur. James McAbram. p. 18

9 March 1803. Levi BURTON and Elizabeth Lansford, dau. of Isham Lansford who consents. Polley Lansford also signed the consent. Sur. Richard Quinty. Married by Rev. Clement Nance. p. 34

15 November 1798. Robert BURTON and Elizabeth Burnett, dau. of Thomas Burnett who consents. Sur. Thomas Stewart. Married by Rev. William Wright. p. 25

3 January 1797. Thomas BURTON and Zeriah McDaniel, dau. of James McDaniel who consents. James Burton, dather of Thomas also consents. Sur. William Brock. p. 23

10 February 1803. George BUTCHER and Sally Barrot. Married by Rev. Griffith Dickinson. p. 34

26 April 1794. Zachariah BUTT and Elizabeth Prewett, dau. of Samuel Prewett who consents. Sur. Bazell Hawker. Married by Rev. Richard Elliott. p. 18

16 July 1804. Matthew CABANESS and Patsey Robertson. Sur. William Smith. Married by Rev. Richard Elliott. p. 36

25 December 1795. Peter CAHALL and Molley Robertson. Sur.
James Robertson. p. 20

10 December 1797. Allen CALDWELL and Polley Tanner, dau. of
Matthew Tanner who consents. Sur. Creed Tanner. Married by Rev.
Lazarus Dodson. p. 23

20 December 1790. David CALDWELL and Elizabeth Tanner. Sur.
Natthew Tanner. Married by Rev. Lazarus Dodson. p. 12

18 October 1790. John CALL and Lucinda Williams. Sur. Richard
Venable. Married by Rev. Lazarus Dodson. p. 12

22 August 1787. Daniel CALLAHAN and Wilmoth Russell. Sur.
Robert Mickelborough. Married by Rev. Lazarus Dodson. p. 9

14 February 1805. Henry G. CALLOWAY and Anna B. Callands, dau.
of Samuel Callands who consents. Sur. William Callands. p. 38

8 January 1805. William CALLOWAY and Elizabeth Callands, dau.
of Samuel Callands who consents. Sur. Henry G. Calloway. p. 38

-- March 1784. Henry CAMMELL and Elizabeth Burges. Married by
Rev. John Bailey. Shouldn't this be Campbell? p. 5

16 December 1805. George CAMPBELL and Patsey Dodson, dau. of
Micajah and Tabitha Dodson who consent. Sur. William Philippin.
Married by Rev. James Nelson. p. 39

23 June 1787. John CAMPBELL and Catharine Leprade, dau. of
Benjamin Leprade who consents. Sur. Joseph Akin. Married by
Rev. David Barr. p. 9

11 September 1802. Richard CAMPBELL and Susannah Elliott. Sur.
Richard Elliott. p. 32

7 July 1782. Cade CAN and Nancy Benton. Married by Rev. John
Bailey. p. 5

1 February 1795. Charles Ewell CARTER and Kezey Walters, dau.
of John Walters who consents. Sur. John Twedell. Married by
Rev. John Atkinson. p. 20

13 February 1799. James CARTER and Amy Motley. Consent of
Joseph Motley. Sur. David Motley. Married by Rev. John
Atkinson. p. 26

10 November 1800. Jeduthan CARTER, Jr., and Beckey Rogers,
dau. of Joseph Rogers who consents and is surety. Married by
Rev. Clement Nance. p. 28

6 February 1797. Jesse CARTER and Susanna Adkins. Sur. Edward
Adkins. p. 23

14

20 September 1796.   John CARTER and Rozanna Reiger.   Sur. Joseph
Akin.   Jacob Reiger consents for Rozanna.   Married by Rev.
Clement Nance.   p. 22

7 February 1795.   Leven CARTER and Elizabeth Womack.   Sur. Allen
Waddill.   p. 20

18 July 1803.   Nathan CARTER and Elizabeth Atkins.   Sur. Henry
Atkins.   Married by Rev. Richard Elliott.   p. 34

7 November 1799.   Taliferro CARTER and Kitty Astin.   Sur. Tolover
Carter.   p. 26

27 January 1792.   William CARVER and Sythe Gowing.   Sur. William
Williams.   p. 15

-- ---- 1799.· Thiel CAWLEY and Barbary Curry.   Married by Rev.
Richard Elliott.   p. 26

14 December 1776.   Samuel CELLAND and Elizabeth Smith, sister
of Ralph Smith who consents.   Sur. John Cox.   p. 2

17 February 1782.   Thomas CHAMBERS and Sarah Mendike.   Married
by Rev. Samuel Harris.   p. 4

26 December 1805.   Thomas CHAMBERS and Elizabeth Stratton.   Sur.
Jesse Hardey.   Married by Rev. Richard Elliott.   p. 38

19 November 1792.   Charles CHANEY and Christa Holloway, dau.
of James Holloway who consents.   Sur. Moses Chaney.   Married
by Rev. Richard Elliott.   p. 15

28 December 1786.   John CHENEY and Susannah Hill.   Married by
Rev. John Adkerson.   p. 8

15 August 1791.   Moses CHANEY and Margaret Davis.   Sur. Thomas
H. Wooding.   Married by Rev. John Atkinson.   p. 14

21 December 1801.   Thomas CHANEY and Elizabeth Dodson, dau. of
George and Elizabeth R. Dodson who consent.   Sur. John Dodson.
Married by Rev. Elias Dodson.   p. 31

6 January 1800.   William CHANEY and Dicey Dodson, dau. of Joshua
Dodson who consents.   Sur. Allen Dodson.   p. 28

19 April 1803.   John CHATTEN, Jr., and Catherine Davis.   Sur.
William Davis.   Married by Rev. Richard Elliott.   p. 34

20 March 1781.   Abia CHEATHAM and Frances McK-----.   Sur.
Henry Mickelburrough.   p. 3

18 July 1795.   Bennett CHELTON and Maryan Ausling.   Sur. Joab
Meadows.   Consent of John Tonson, step-father.   (For which one?)
p. 20

2 December 1795. Joshua CHILDRESS and Frankey Crane, dau. of John Crain who consents. Sur. Richard Proctor. Married by Rev. Richard Elliott. p. 20

-- ---- 1799. Robert CHILDRESS and Polley Turley. Married by Rev. Richard Elliott. p. 26

19 January 1789. William CHILDRESS and Rebecca Ford. Sur. James Martin Williams. Married by Rev. Lazarus Dodson. p. 11

18 July 1791. Bennett CHILTON and Mary Ann Ausling. Married by Rev. John Atkinson. p. 14

19 November 1798. Lawrence CLAPS and Molley Cline. Sur. John Dalton. Married by Rev. Thomas Payne. p. 25

14 November 1791. John CLARK and Polly Wilson, dau. of Peter Wilson who consents. Sur. T. Wilson, Jr. Shouldn't this be P. Wilson, Jr.? p. 14

18 February 1799. John CLARK and Jane Cook Wilson. Sur. Josiah Earp. p. 26

18 January 1798. Leonard CLARK and Mary Burgess, dau. of William Burgess who consents. Sur. Zachariah Prewett. Married by Rev. William Wright. p. 25

25 December 1795. Moses CLARK and Sarah Pemberton, dau. of John Pemberton who consents. Sur. Nathaniel Luck. Married by Rev. James Kinney. p. 20

21 March 1803. Peter CLARK and Elizabeth Campbell. Sur. John Campbell, Jr. p. 34

11 November 1805. Thomas CLARK and Drucilla Earp, dau. of Josiah Earp who consents. Sur. Berryman Dalton. Married by Rev. George Dodson. p. 39

21 June 1784. William CLARK and Jane White. Sur. William White. Married by Rev. David Barr. p. 5

20 August 1787. William CLARK and Jane Anne Shelton. Sur. Armistead Shelton. Married by Rev. James Hinton. p. 9

5 January 1790. William CLARK and Betsey Ballinger. Sur. John Ballinger. Married by Rev. James Kinney. p. 12

24 January 1805. William CLARK and Polley Brown. Married by Rev. Griffith Dickinson. p. 38

3 December 1788. Matthew CLAY and Mary Williams. Sur. Walter Samuel. Married by Rev. James Hilton. Signs her own consent. p. 10

17 April 1786. Benjamin CLEMENT and Sariah (Sarah?) Bailey.
Sur. Joshua Abston. p. 8

9 December 1802. Hugh CLEMENTS and Mary Keatt. Married by
Rev. Griffith Dickinson. p. 32

-- ---- 1800. William CLEMMANS and Elizabeth Goard. Married
by Rev. Thomas Douglas. p. 28

15 November 1790. Vachel CLEMENTS and Lucretia Lewis, dau. of
Charles Lewis who consents. Sur. Edward Lewis. p. 12

7 March 1793. Stephen CLEVER and Elizabeth Crawford. Sur.
Thomas Corbin. Signs her own consent. Married by Rev. Matthew
Bates. p. 17

21 October 1802. Thomas CLIFF and Jaenea Delosiea. Married
by Rev. Clement Nance. p. 32

28 August 1791. Joseph CLIFT and Sarah Pearson. Sur. John
Pearson. p. 14

25 October 1788. John CLOPTON and Jane Perkins. Jeny Perkins
consents for Jane. Sur. Thomas Linthicum, Jr. p. 10

26 August 1784. Redmond CODY and Elizabeth Davis, dau. of
Thomas Davis who consents. Sur. John George. p. 5

1 May 1795. Person COE and Jane Flowers. Married by Rev.
John Jenkins. p. 20

12 July 1794. Barnett COLE and Priscilla Ferguson, dau. of
Nathaniel Ferguson who consents. Sur. Nathan Cunningham.
Married by Rev. Richard Elliott. p. 18

2 December 1805. David COLE and Elizabeth Cornwell, dau. of
Francis Cornwell who consents. Sur. Fourshee C. Cornwell.
Married by Rev. Elias Dodson. p. 38

10 December 1796. Jeremiah COLE and Nancy Tanner, dau. of
Matthew Tanner, Jr., who consents. Sur. Nathan Cunningham.
Married by Rev. Lazarus Dodson. p. 22

26 August 1787. Richard COLE and Nancy Shackelford, dau. of
Eunice Shackelford who consents. Sur. Ezekiel Russell. p. 9

21 December 1804. Tunas COLE and Nancy Cunningham. Sur. David
Cole. Nathan Cunningham consents for Nancy. p. 36

6 January 1803. William COLE and Lucy Cunningham. Nathan
Cunningham consents for Lucy Sur. David Cole. Married by
Rev. James Nelson. p. 34

5 March 1797. Daniel COLEMAN and Polley Coleman, dau. of Stephen Coleman who consents. Sur. Daniel Price. p. 23

21 November 1798. Daniel COLEMAN and Anna Payne Harrison, dau. of William Harrison who consents. Sur. Clement McDaniel. p. 25

6 December 1771. Spilsby COLEMAN and Judith Burton, dau. of Robert Burton who consents. Sur. Benjamin Terry. p. 1

3 September 1799. Stephen COLEMAN and Polley Williams, dau. of Permeneas Williams who consents. Sur. Daniel Coleman. p. 26

-- April 1791. John COLLEY and Frances Holloway. Sur. James Holloway. Married by Rev. Richard Elliott. p. 14

12 June 1801. James COLLIE and Nancy Jennings, dau. of Robert and Susannah Jennings who consent. Sur. Charles Collie. Married by Rev. Elias Dodson. p. 31

4 January 1793. Ambrose COLLIER and Elizabeth McDowell, dau. of William McDowell who consents. Sur. James Dalton. p. 17

10 November 1795. Laban COMBS and Peggey Harris, dau. of Joseph and Laney Harris who consent. Sur. Isham Lansford. Married by Rev. Clement Nance. p. 20

19 December 1804. John COMPTON and Lucey Tapleigh. Sur. Obediah Ham. Signs her own consent. Married by Rev. John Jenkins. p. 36

21 January 1791. Levy COMPTON and Patsey Owen. Sur. John Owen. p. 14

-- ---- 1804. William COMPTON and Susanna Bayless. Married by Rev. John Jenkins. p. 36

9 December 1802. John CONNER and Polley Thompson. Sur. Samuel Thompson. Married by Rev. Griffith Dickinson. p. 32

2 January 1799. Christopher CONWAY and Anna Slayden, dau. of Daniel Slayden who consents. Sur. John Slayden. Married by Rev. John Atkinson. p. 26

-- ---- 1805. Harmon COOK and Catharine Whitsell. Married by Rev. Richard Elliott. p. 38

4 February 1786. Herman COOK, Jr., and Susannah Ramsey, dau. of Thomas Ramsey who consents. Sur. Woodson Ramsey. Married by Rev. David Barr. p. 8

5 April 1787. Jacob COOLEY, Jr., and Nancy Gover. Married by Rev. David Barr. p. 9

14 December 1802. Charles COOPER and Anne Terry. Sur. John
Terry. Signs her own consent. p. 32

17 July 1804. James CORBIN and Milley Wright, dau. of George
Wright who consents. Sur. David Corbin. Married by Rev. Richard
Elliott. p. 36

16 November 1795. Thomas CORBIN and Susanna Claybourn. Sur.
Joseph Ryburn. Signs her own consent. Married by Rev. Richard
Elliott. p. 20

27 February 1786. William CORBIN and Susanna Davis. Married
by Rev. Lazarus Dodson. p. 8 (Must be an error for 1787)

19 February 1787. William CORBIN and Susannah Davis. Consent
of William Davis. Sur. Samuel Parks. p. 9

-- ---- 1785. Jpehthan CORNELIUS and Peggey Everet. Married
by Rev. Nathaniel Thurman. p. 7

5 April 1785. James COLQUIT and Margaret Hampton. Married by
Rev. Thomas Sparks. p. 7

19 February 1795. William COTTERALL and Rachel Richards.
Married by Rev. Richard Elliott. p. 20

3 October 1777. Edward COVINGTON and Frances Pruitt. Sur.
James Austin. Signs her own consent. p. 2

20 January 1793. John COVINGTON and Jane Hankins. Sur.
William Hankins. p. 17

12 January 1805. William COVINGTON and Caty Roberts. Sur.
Reubin Hankins. p. 39

4 October 1790. James COX and Elizabeth I. Hankins. Sur.
Joseph Akin. p. 12

11 January 1800. Lewis COX and Nancy Shaw, dau. of Thomas and
Jean Shaw who consent. Sur. Robert Shaw. p. 28

3 November 1800. Philip COX and Polley Watson, dau. of James
Watson who consents. Sur. John Bennett. p. 28

12 September 1781. John CRADDOCK and Mary Hendricks. Sur.
Nathan Hendricks. p. 3

25 September 1796. Richard CRADDOCK and Ann Bumpass, dau. of
William Bumpass who consents. Sur. Robert Bumpass. Married
by Rev. John Jenkins. p. 22

27 August 1805. Samuel CRADDOCK and Elizabeth Warren, dau.
of Henry Warren who consents. Sur. John Warren. p. 39

8 January 1803. George CRAFT and Milley Parker, dau. of William Parker who consents and is surety. p. 34

.5 November 1798. Philip CRAFT and Nancy Parker, dau. of William Parker who consents and is surety. Married by Rev. James Tompkins. p. 25

21 September 1791. Thomas CRAIG and Mary Wisdom. Married by Rev. Lazarus Dodson. p. 14

17 September 1787. Glover CRAIN and Tabitha Rowden. Sur. John Rowden. Married by Rev. James Hinton. p. 9

11 February 1794. James CRANE and Anne Price. Married by Rev. Richard Elliott. p. 18

14 October 1800. William CRANE and Polley Vaden. Sur. Wilson Vaden. p. 28

22 December 1782. David CRAWFORD and Christian Terry. Married by Rev. John Bailey. p. 4

22 December 1782. Moses CRAWFORD and Susannah Willis. Married by Rev. John Bailey. p. 4

5 October 1800. Strother CRAWFORD and Nancy Hutison. Sur. Wilson Vaden. Married by Rev. Richard Elliott. p. 28

3 January 1803. Elijah CREEL and Nancy Ragland, dau. of Gideon Ragland. Sur. Walker Goodwin. p. 34

17 April 1797. John CREEL and Margaret Dodson, dau. of Lazarus Dodson who consents. Sur. John Dodson. Married by Rev. George Dodson. p. 23

16 May 1803. William CREMER and Yuleanna Rider. Sur. Jacob Crider. Married by Rev. Thomas Payne. p. 34

-- ---- 1805. James CRENSHAW and Betsey Newbil. Married by Rev. George Dodson. p. 38

26 May 1804. Robert CRENSHAW and Mary Shelton. Sur. Armistead Shelton. Married by Rev. Griffith Dickinson. p. 36

18 February 1787. William Winston CRENSHAW and Sarah Kirby, dau. of John Kirby who consents. Sur. Nathaniel Kirby. Married by Rev. David Barr. p. 5

13 November 1805. George CREWS and Pheba Culley. Sur. Samuel Hailey. Jesse Cruse signs certificate. Married by Rev. George Dodson. p. 38

11 September 1802. Thomas CREWS and Patty Saunders, dau. of John and Mary Sanders who consent. Sur. Joseph Yates. p. 32

10 December 1798. William CREWS and Nancey Martin, dau. of Eleanor Martin who consents. Sur. Benjamin Martin. Married by Rev. John Jenkins. p. 25

18 November 1805. William CREWS and Patsey Hains. Sur. John Shields. Signs her own consent. p. 38

1 January 1796. Andrew CRIDER and Christina Debo, dau. of Philip Debo who consents. Sur. Abraham Debo. p. 22

31 March 1790. Daniel CRIDER, Jr., and Nancy Bennett, dau. of Thomas and Peggy Bennett who consent. Sur. Elijah Bennett. Married by Rev. Thomas Douglas. p. 12

3 January 1803. George CRIDER and Frances Bennett, dau. of Thomas F. Bennett who consents. Sur. Henry Crider. Married by Rev. Elias Dodson. p. 34

-- ---- 1800. Jacob CRIDER and Mary Riter. Married by Rev. Thomas Douglas. p. 28

21 December 1801. Jacob CROFF and Polley Kezee, dau. of John Kezee who consents. Sur. Richard Kezee. Married by Rev. Thomas Payne. p. 31

20 July 1787. Drury CROSS and Martha Oliver, dau. of William Oliver who consents. Sur. John Stocktone. Married by Rev. David Barr. p. 9

8 August 1792. William CROSS and Mary Oliver, dau. of William Oliver who consents. Sur. Joseph Fuller. Married by Rev. Clement Nance. p. 15

20 October 1794. John CROUCH and Susannah Williams, dau. of Charles Williams who consents. Sur. William Astin. Married by Rev. Thomas Sparks. p. 18

16 April 1795. Sibert CRUTCHER and Sarah Gilbert. Married by Rev. John Jenkins. p. 20

13 January 1803. John CRYDER and Catey Croff, dau. of Jacob Groff who consents. Sur. Samuel Cryder. Married by Rev. Thomas Payne. p. 34

12 December 1792. Elijah CUMMINGS and Salley Astin. Sur. John May. Married by Rev. Matthew Bates. p. 15

6 October 1792. Joseph CUNNINGHAM and Elizabeth Cunningham. Sur. Jeremiah Gray. Consent of Thomas Cunningham, father (of which one? Probably Elizabeth). p. 15

28 September 1789. William CUNNINGHAM and Margaret Dean. Married by Rev. Richard Elliott. p. 11

16 May 1798. Thomas CURREY and Peggy Hankins, dau. of William Hankins who consents. Sur. William Pearson. Married by Rev. Clement Nance. p. 25

11 February 1796. Barth. CURRY and Rozanna Nuckols. Sur. Josiah Nuckols. Married by Rev. Richard Elliott. p. 22

19 January 1795. Israel CURRY and Sally Payne. Sur. Joseph Curry. p. 20

24 March 1785. Isaac CURRY and Rhoda Grisham. Married by Rev. David Barr. p. 7

9 December 1790. Nathan CURRY and Nancy Grisham. Married by Rev. Clement Nance. p. 12

13 November 1802. Thomas CURRY and Nancy Crane, dau. of Susanna Crain who consents. Sur. William Curry. Married by Rev. Richard Elliott. p. 32

-- ---- 180-. William CURRY and Patsey Jeffress, dau. of John Jeffress who consents. Sur. Thomas Curry. Married by Rev. Richard Elliott who says Jeffreys. p. 28

17 July 1802. Samuel DABNEY and Mildred Hopson. Joseph Hopson, guardian of Mildred consents. Sur. James Dix. p. 33

21 September 1801. William DABNEY and Nancey Lindsay. Sur. Severn Busey. p. 31

9 December 1795. Jesse DAILEY and Polley Turner, dau. of Pierce F. Turner who consents. Sur. Edward Popejoy. p. 20

-- ---- 1800. John DAILEY and Polley Compton. Married by Rev. John Jenkins. p. 28

12 April 1801. Hugh DALEY and Elizabeth Church, dau. of Jonathan Church, Sr., who consents. Sur. Jonathan Church, Jr. Married by Rev. Thomas Sparks. p. 31

11 November 1803. Benjamin DALTON and Caty Mayhue. Sur. Drury Owen. Married by Rev. Griffith Dickinson. p. 34

19 December 1805. Berryman DALTON and Sarah Cook, step-dau. of John Clark and dau. of Jean Clark who consent. Sur. William Bryant. Married by Rev. George Dodson. p. 39

10 March 1804. Eligy DALTON and Nancy Brogin. Sur. Lewis Dalton. Signs her own consent. p. 36

19 January 1795. Isham DALTON and Mary Goad, dau. of Charles and Rachel Goad who consent. Sur. Samuel Dalton. Married by Rev. Joseph Drury. p. 20

18 April 1782. James DALTON and Agness Dyer. Married by Rev. John Bailey. p. 4

19 January 1791. James DALTON and Agatha Patterson. Sur. Ambrose Dalton. Signs her own consent. p. 14

5 September 1804. James DALTON and Molley Dalton. Sur. John McCrickett. Married by Rev. Joseph Hatchett. p. 36

26 December 1804. Jesse DALTON and Catharine Clark, dau. of John Clark who consents. Sur. Thomas Clark. Married by Rev. George Dodson. p. 36

15 July 1788. John DALTON and Luvania Picknall. Sur. John Dalton. p. 10

12 November 1797. Lewis DALTON and Mary Keezee. Married by Rev. Thomas Payne. p. 23

11 June 1801. Lewis DALTON and Betsey Chambers. Sur. Benjamin Dalton. p. 31

20 June 1803. Martin DALTON and Caty Crider, dau. of Daniel Crider who consents. Sur. Samuel Crider. Married by Rev. Thomas Payne. p. 34

22 September 1767. Samuel DALTON, Jr. and Charlotte Gallihue, dau. of William Gallihue and his wife, Anne Kenner. Sur. John Wimbish. p. 1

-- ---- 1788. Thomas DALTON and Elizabeth Patterson. Married by Rev. James Kinney. p. 10

17 November 1804. William DALTON and Winifred Foster. Sur. John Oneal. George Dalton father of William. Married by Rev. Thomas Sparks. p. 36

17 December 1798. Winston DALTON and Sarah Pullin. Sur. Alexander Bennett. p. 25

18 October 1786. John DAVIDSON and Rachel Chilton. Married by Rev. John Adkerson. p. 8

31 January 1800. Benjamin DAVIS and Lidy Meador, dau. of Joel Meadow who consents. Sur. John Davis. p. 28

4 October 1794. George DAVIS and Mary Tribble, dau. of Susanne Tribble who consents. Sur. Matt Mays. Married by Rev. Matthew Bates. p. 18

12 December 1793. Isaac DAVIS and Polley Denton, dau. of James Denton who consents. Sur. Abner McDowell. p. 17

24 January 1797. James DAVIS and Any Gray. Sur. Joshua Gray. Jeremiah Gray signs certificate. p. 23

12 April 1790. John DAVIS and Nancy Jones, dau. of Huriah Jones who consents. Sur. Thomas Landford. p. 12

26 September 1803. John DAVIS, Jr., and Nancy Hodnett. Sur. Joseph Davis. Married by Rev. Richard Elliott. p. 34

19 March 1793. Joseph DAVIS and Lucy Hodnett. Sur. John Hodnett. Married by Rev. Lazarus Dodson. p. 17

19 November 1798. Joseph DAVIS and Mercy Beck, dau. of William and Lucy Beck who consent. Sur. Richard Beck. Married by Rev. Clement Nance. p. 25

21 July 1802. Nelson DAVIS and Martha Epperson. Sur. Theo. Haley. Signs her own consent. p. 33

13 January 1794. Thomas DAVIS and Jane Hodnett. Sur. John Hodnett. Married by Rev. Lazarus Dodson. p. 18

8 July 1797. Thomas DAVIS and Sally Meadows. Sur. Samuel Meadows. Married by Rev. John Atkinson. p. 24

23 September 1800. William DAVIS and Nancy Jenkins. John Jenkins consents for Nancy. Sur. Samuel Goodman. Married by Rev. John Jenkins. p. 28

8 May 1804. William DAVIS and Lucey Meade. Sur. Meredith Meade. Married by Rev. Richard Elliott. p. 36

30 July 1781. Brooks DAWSON and Ann Jones, dau. of Thomas Jones who consents and is surety. p. 3

17 August 1801. William DAY and Polley Formby, dau. of Nathan Formby who consents. Sur. Martin Farmer. p. 31

14 September 1788. Gilbert DEAR and Anne Norton, dau. of John Morton, Sr., who consents. Sur. Thomas Oliver. p. 10

14 November 1797. Abraham DEBO and Sarah Smith. Sur. Hezekiah Barber. p. 23

3 January 1795. Michael DEBO and Catherine Sanders. Sur. Jacob Sanders. p. 20

17 June 1799. Philip DEBO and Eleanor Smith, dau. of William Smith who consents. Sur. James Nowlin. p. 26

7 October 1805. Samuel DENNERSON and Hetta Lay. Sur. Richard Ramsey. Benjamin Dennerson father of Samuel, signs certificate. p. 39

4 October 1803. William DENNERSON and Jenny Barron, dau. of Josiah Barron who consents and is surety. Married by Rev. James Nelson. p. 34

16 December 1805. Zachariah DENNERSON and Milley Phillips, dau. of Molley Phillips who consents. Sur. Benjamin Dennerson. Married by Rev. George Dodson. p. 39

15 .October 1804. John DENNISON and Barbara Wigell. Sur. Nichos Tree. p. 36

25 August 1800. Joseph DENTON and Polley Hudson, dau. of John M. Hutson who consents. Sur. Joseph Hudson. Married by Rev. John Wyatt. p. 28

10 July 1795. Alexander DEVIN and Lukey Nowlin. Sur. Edward Nunnelee. Byron W. Nowlin consents for Lukey. Married by Rev. Richard Elliott. p. 20

-- ---- 1800. Alexander DEVIN and Susanna Nowlin. Married by Rev. Thomas Douglas. p. 38

13 August 1803. James DEVIN and Peggy Thomas, dau. of Jonathan Thomas who consents. Sur. William Biggers. p. 34

16 February 1789. Joseph DEVIN and Elizabeth Nowling. Sur. William Devin. Married by Rev. Richard Elliott. p. 11

22 January 1791. Robert DEVIN and Nancy Parrish, dau. of Joseph Parrish who consents. Sur. Joseph Akin. Married by Rev. Richard Elliott. p. 14

30 October 1804. Benjamin DODD and Susanna Goodman. Sur. Edmund Goodman. Married by Rev. Griffith Dickinson. p. 36

5 November 1802. Nathaniel DODD and Betsey Perkins, dau.,of Mary Perkins who consents. Sur. Robert Scales. Married by Rev. Clement Nance. p. 32

10 October 1800. Absolom DODSON and Anna Morris. Sur. William Morris. Married by Rev. John Jenkins. p. 28

19 December 1782. David DODSON and Frances Fitzgerald. Sur. Joseph Dodson. Married by Rev. John Bailey. p. 4

23 November 1785. Elias DODSON and Nancy Stamps. Married by Rev. Lazarus Dodson. p. 7

19 April 1787. George DODSON and Hannah Wall, dau. of Charles Wall who consents. Sur. John Bennett. Married by Rev. John Adkinson. p. 9

-- ---- 1805. George DODSON and Ludy Dodson. Married by Rev. John Atkinson. p. 39

7 January 1804. Hightower DODSON and Unity Dodson. Sur. David Dodson. Married by Rev. Elias Dodson. p. 36

23 January 1798. John DODSON and Nancy Madding, dau. of John Madding who consents. Sur. Robert Madding. Married by Rev. Lazarus Dodson. p. 25

21 September 1779. Joshua DODSON and Ann Shelton, dau. of Charles Shelton who consents. Sur. Thomas Tunstall. p. 2

3 April 1787. Micajah DODSON and Tabitha Dodson, dau. of S. Dodson who consents. Sur. W. Wright. p. 9

24 February 1798. Ralph DODSON and Elizabeth Bennett. Sur. Travis Bennett. Signs her own consent. Married by Rev. Lazarus Dodson. p. 25

16 December 1799. Samuel DODSON and Polley King. Sur. Fortunand Dodson. p. 26

19 July 1794. William DODSON and Tabitha Hendrick, dau. of Humphrey Hendrick who consents. Sur. John Bennett. Married by Rev. John Atkinson. p. 18

-- ---- 1796. William DODSON and Tabitha Hendrick. Married by Rev. John Atkinson. p. 22

17 August 1779. John DONELSON and Mary Purnell. Sur. Joseph Akin. Signs her own consent. p. 2

19 July 1790. Ambrose DOSS and Sarah Thurman. Richard Thurman consents for Sarah. Sur. John Thacker. Married by Rev. James Kinney. p. 12

15 August 1804. James DOSS and Arabella Hundley, dau. of Joseph Hundley who consents. Sur. Arch Hundley. p. 37

13 August 1793. Jesse DOSS and Rachel Brooks, dau. of Samuel and Mary Brooks who consent. Sur. Drury Owen. Married by Rev. Matthew Bates. p. 17

-- ---- 1785. John DOSS and Mary Shields. Married by Rev. Nathaniel Thurman. p. 7

24 January 1802. John DOSS and ---- ----. Sur. William Hodges. p. 33

12 January 1792. David DOTSON and Frances Fitzgerald. Married by Rev. Lazarus Dodson. p. 15

19 December 1791. Joseph DOTSON and Sarah Richardson. Sur. David Dotson. Married by Rev. John Atkinson. p. 14

23 May 1793. John DOUGLASS and Mary Browner. Married by Rev. Lazarus Dodson. p. 17

21 November 1803. John DOUGLAS and Elizabeth McDaniel, dau. of Clement McDaniel who consents. Sur. Stockley Turner. Married by Rev. Griffith Dickinson. p. 34

27 April 1789. Elijah DOVE and Massy Kendrick, dau. of Thomas and Sarah Kendrick who consent. Sur. Joseph Akin. Married by Rev. Richard Elliott. p. 11

17 December 1804. George DOVE and Caty Bruce. Sur. James Bruce. Married by Rev. Griffith Dickinson. p. 36

20 August 1804. David DICKINSON and Nancy Oakes. Sur. Isaac Potter. Married by Rev. William Davis. p. 36

12 October 1785. Griffith DICKINSON and Susanna Shelton, dau. of Crispin Shelton who consents. Sur. James Akin. p. 7

9 May 1795. William DICKSON and Sarah Smith. Sur. John Gammon. Patte Smith consents for Sarah. Married by Rev. Clement Nance. p. 20

20 June 1782. John DINNEY and Elizabeth Holder. Married by Rev. John Bailey. p. 4

24 March 1785. John DIX and Betsey Lumpkins. Married by Rev. Samuel Harris. p. 7

15 January 1781. William DIX and Rebeckah Booker. Sur. Joseph Akin. p. 3

6 July 1787. William DIX and Patsey Hendrick, dau. of Humphrey Hendrick who consents. Sur. W. Wright. Married by Rev. Lazarus Dodson. p. 9

8 January 1786. Wynne DIXON and Ketturah Payne. Married by Rev. Samuel Harris. p. 8

3 April 1802. William DRAINE and Nancy Earls. Sur. Drury Oliver. Married by Rev. Clement Nance. p. 33

10 October 1793. William DRANE and Nancy Smithe. Sur. William Smithe. Married by Rev. Matthew Bates. p. 17

2 February 1770. Thomas DUDLEY and Savannah Burton. Sur.
Dudley Gatewood. Signs her own consent. p. 1

9 February 1782. Lawrence DUFF and Elizabeth Willis. Married
by Rev. John Bailey. p. 4

1 May 1784. Jesse DUNCAN and Anne Pigg. Sur. Joseph Akin. p. 5

18 December 1788. Francis DUNCARD and Sarah Ellinton. Married
by Rev. Lazarus Dodson. p. 10

24 October 1782. Samuel DUMKIN and Mary Samson. Married
by Rev. John Bailey. p. 4

4 January 1802. James DUNN and Dicey Martin. Sur. John
Martin. Signs her own consent. p. 33

12 May 1802. William DUNN and Martha Kerby. Sur. James Dunn.
John Dunn father of William. Married by Rev. Thomas Payne.
p. 32

28 June 1785. James DUNNING and Mary Marlow. Sur. Arthur
Keesee. Signs her own consent. Married by Rev. John Bailey.
p. 7

24 November 1802. William DUNNING and Sarah Coe. Married by
Rev. Griffith Dickinson. p. 32

7 April 1787. William DUPEE and Sarah Blair. Sarah Dupee
mother of William consents. Sur. W. Wright. Married by Rev.
Lazarus Dodson. p. 9

9 June 1788. John DUPREY and Sallie Walker Stokes, dau. of
Sillas Stokes who consents. Sur. Allen Stokes. p. 10

9 July 1787. John DYER, Jr., and Viney Morton, dau. of John
Morton who consents. Sur. James Dyer. Married by Rev. David
Barr. p. 9

3 June 1801. John DYER and Mary Nash (widow). Sur. Luther
Hopper. Signs her own consent. p. 31

-- ---- 1788. Nathan DYER and Nancy Dalton. Married by Rev.
Richard Elliott. p. 10

15 February 1793. Nathan DYER and Mary Payne. Sur. William
T. Gauldin. p. 17

11 October 1796. William DYER and Nancy Ward. Sur. Robert
Devin. Edward Popjoy consents for Nancy. Married by Rev.
James Tompkins. p. 22

20 September 1802. William DYER and Ann Shelton. Sur. Isham
Burton. p. 32

21 November 1803. William DYER and Polley Alexander, dau. of
William Alexander who consents. Sur. Lawson H. Carter. Married
by Rev. Thomas Payne. p. 34

27 September 1802. Joseph Alford EADS and Judah Doss, dau.
of Thomas Doss who consents. Sur. John Eads. p. 33

24 August 1802. Samuel EARLS and Sally Mullins, dau. of Thomas
Mullins who consents. Sur. Henry Richardson. Married by
Rev. Clement Nance. p. 33

22 November 1798. Nimrod EARP and Priscilla Cook. Sur. Philip
Earp. George Cook consents for Priscilla. Married by Rev.
William Wright. p. 25

17 August 1792. Samuel EARP and Elizabeth Cook, dau. of George
Cook who consents. Sur. Josiah Earp. p. 15

16 January 1804. Pyrant EASLEY and Sarah Crenshaw. Sur.
Joseph Carter. Signs her own consent. Married by Rev. David
Nowlin. p. 37

21 February 1785. William EASLEY and Sarah Lester. Sur.
Blanks Moody and I.L. Baker. p. 6

8 November 1797. Ezekiel EAST and Elizabeth Worsham. Married
by Rev. James Kinney. p. 24

-- ---- 1799. Isaac EAST and Joicey Pemberton. Married by
Rev. John Jenkins. p. 26

19 May 1794. William ECHOLS and Mary Farmer. Sur. Isham
Farmer. p. 18

18 January 1799. Evans ECHOLS and Anna Terry. Consent of
Elizabeth Terry. Sur. Martin Farmer. p. 26

11 February 1797. Moses ECHOLS and Betsey Terry. Sur. David
Williams. Signs her own consent. Married by Rev. Richard
Elliott. p. 24

18 March 1799. Moses ECHOLS and Sally Farmer. Sur. Isham
Farmer. Married by Rev. John Jenkins. p. 26

5 July 1791. Obediah ECHOLS and Betsy Terry. Sur. Jonas
Meadows. Signs her own consent. Married by Rev. John
Atkinson. p. 14

-- ---- 1790. John EDS and Patsy Ingram. Married by Rev.
John Jenkins. p. 12

10 November 1805. Daniel ELDER and Mary Coe, dau. of Francis
P. and Nancy Coe who consent. Mary also signs consent. Sur.
William Coe. Married by Rev. Griffith Dickinson. p. 39

29

29 February 1780. Enock Ward ELLINGTON and Judith Woodson, dau. of Tucker Woodson who consents. Sur. James Farmer. p. 3

2 March 1779. Ward ELLINGTON and Sarah Woodson. Sur. Tucker Woodson. p. 2

3 January 1800. Daniel ELLIOTT and Polley Bailey, dau. of Peter J. Bailey who consents. Sur. John Bailey. Married by Rev. Richard Elliott. p. 28

6 February 1794. James ELLIOTT and Sarah Shumake. Sur. Joshua Prenett. Married by Rev. Thomas Sparks. p. 18

30 December 1805. James ELLIOTT and Sally Polley. Sur. John Polley. Married by Rev. Richard Elliott. p. 39

21 December 1803. John ELLIOTT and Judith Williams. Sur. Thomas Allsup. p. 34

28 May 1800. Jonathan ELLIOTT and Rebekah Ward. Sur. Thomas Blakeley. p. 28

19 November 1798. Samuel ELLIOTT and Milley Boaz, dau. of Agness Boaz who consents. Sur. Daniel Boaz. Married by Rev. James Tompkins. p. 25

23 April 1805. Simon ELLIOTT and Constance Williams. Sur. Thomas Alsup. p. 39

21 January 1804. Thomas ELLIOTT and Polley Ragadale, step-dau. of William Ross and dau. of Mary Ross who consent. Sur. Josiah Shelton. Married by Rev. Thomas Sparks. p. 37

28 October 1794. William ELLIOTT and Sibbe Williams. Sur. James Elliott. Benjamin Williams consents for Sibbe. Married by Rev. Richard Elliott. p. 18

-- ---- 1783. Jesse EMMERSON and Elizabeth Emmerson. Married by Rev. John Bailey. p. 5

6 October 1804. Francis EPPERSON and Jincey Mitchel. Sur. Michael Mitchel. Married by Rev. John Jenkins. p. 37

18 March 1800. John EPPERSON and Sarah Thomas (widow). Sur. William Tullock. Signs her own consent. Married by Rev. Richard Elliott. p. 28

20 August 1804. William EPPERSON and Maryann Colligan. Sur. Samuel Fuqua. Signs her own consent. Married by Rev. John Jenkins. p. 37

14 November 1782. William ERVET and Anney Richards. Married by Rev. Lazarus Dodson. p. 4

9 December 1793.   Joel ESTES and Rachel Ward.   Sur. Joseph Akin.   Married by Rev. John King.   p. 17

18 March 1805.   William EVANS and Sarah Shelton.   Sur. Langston Brown.   Married by Rev. Richard Elliott.   p. 39

15 December 1784.   Charles EVENS and Susanna Mackey.   Married by Rev. Thomas Sparks.   p. 5

8 April 1793.   Eppy EVERETT and Catharine Everett.   Sur. William Everett.   Married by Rev. John W. Jones.   p. 17

20 December 1798.   Eppy EVERETT and Casey Bucey.   Sur. Edward Bucey.   Married by Rev. William Wright.   p. 25

11 March 1799.   Peter FALLING and Rosamond Wright.   Sur. William Wright.   p. 26

23 February 1793.   Redmon FALLON and Elizabeth Gwin, dau. of George Homes Gwin who consents.   Sur. William Southerland.   p. 17

1 December 1780.   Benjamin FARMER and Ermin Herring, dau. of William Herring who consents.   Sur. Lodowick Farmer.   p. 3

8 January 1802.   Hubbard FARMER and Mary Jenkins, dau. of John Jenkins who consents.   Sur. Pleasant Farmer.   p. 33

15 February 1780.   James FARMER and Betsy Hubbard, dau. of Samuel Hubbard who consents.   Sur. Joseph Akin.   p. 3

2 April 1804.   Johnston FARMER and Patsey Thompson, dau. of Charles Thompson who consents.   Sur. Clement Brown.   p. 37

15 September 1788.   Marlin FARMER and Betsey Echols, dau. of Moses Echols who consents.   Sur. James Farmer.   p. 10

-- ---- 1804.   John FARIS and Polley Dawson.   Married by Rev. John Jenkins.   p. 37

29 November 1793.   Nathaniel FARRIS and Frances Roach.   Sur. Leonard Dove.   Signs her own consent.   Married by Rev. Matthew Bates.   p. 17

7 February 1797.   Abner FARTHING and Elley Roberts.   Sur. Dudley Farthing.   Signs her own consent.   Married by Rev. Thomas Payne.   p. 24

17 December 1803.   Dudley FARTHING and Polley Adams, dau. of Nathan Adams who consents.   Sur. John Adams.   Married by Rev. Thomas Payne.   p. 34

26 January 1786.   John FARTHING and Prudence Moore.   Sur. Joseph Akin.   Married by Rev. Samuel Harris.   p. 8

31

17 March 1788. Sandy FARTHING and Margaret Wright. Sur. Richard Farthing. Signs her own consent. p. 10

-- ---- 1800. Solomon FARTHING and Milley Watson. Married by Rev. Richard Elliott. p. 29

-- ---- 1800. Pleasant FEARS and Isabel Childress. Married by Rev. Thomas Douglas. p. 29

26 November 1792. Covington FERGUSON and Frances Gunnell. Sur. Leonard Bell. p. 15

26 December 1788. Joseph FERGUSON and Patsey Vaughan. Sur. William Wilkinson. p. 10

23 November 1793. Nathaniel FERGUSON and Fanny Bridgewater. Sur. Peter James Bailey. Married by Rev. Richard Elliott. p. 17

18 July 1792. John FINNEY and Milley Stewart. Sur. Francis Shaw. p. 15

28 December 1790. Edmund FITZGERALD and Sarah Dodson. Married by Rev. Lazarus Dodson. p. 12

18 November 1803. James FITZGERALD and Fanny Dodson, dau. of Fortune Dodson who consents and is surety. Married by Rev. Elias Dodson. p. 34

17 September 1792. John FITZGERALD and Jane Holloway. Sur. Joseph Akin. Signs her own consent. Married by Rev. Lazarus Dodson. p. 15

9 March 1799. John FITZGERALD and Nelly Dodson. Sur. David Dodson. p. 26

18 December 1804. Walter FITZGERALD and Patsy Harrison, dau. of William Harrison who consents. Sur. Thomas Stamps. p. 37

18 June 1790. Thomas FLETCHER and Keziah Farris, dau. of Joseph Farris who consents. Sur. Joshua Short. Married by Rev. James Hurt. p. 12

16 September 1805. Samuel FLIPPIN and Delah Ann Corbin. Sur. Charles Cornwell. Married by Rev. James Nelson. p. 39

FLIPPIN: See Phlippin

4 January 1791. Thomas FOMBEY and Nancy Thompson, dau. of George Thompson who consents and is surety. Married by Rev. John Atkinson. p. 14

15 March 1804. Abner FOSTER and Judith Lane. Sur. John O. Neal. p. 37

1 February 1800. John FOSTER and Winney Thurman. Sur. Joseph
Thurman. p. 28

21 December 1795. Aaron FOUNBY and Susanna Thompson, dau. of
George Thompson who consents. Sur. Joseph Thompson. Married
by Rev. Samuel D. Brame. p. 20

7 August 1790. John FRASHER and Betsey Lancaster, dau. of
John Lancaster who consents. Sur. William Frasher. Married
by Rev. James Kinney. p. 12

12 December 1782. Peter FREEMAN and Mary Combs. Married by
Rev. John Bailey. p. 4

-- ---- 1788. Isaac FRIZELL and Sarah Williams, dau. of Benjamin
and Anne Williams who consent. p. 10

19 March 1788. Abraham FRIZLE (Frizell) and Sarah Williams.
Sur. George Hill. p. 10

18 February 1799. David FRIZLE and Nancy Ballinger. Sur.
Nathan Frizle. p. 26

17 November 1800. Isaac FRIZZLE and Lydia Boaz, dau. of Agness
Boaz who consents. Sur. Thomas Boaz. p. 28

25 April 1794. Jacob FRIZZLE and Jane Robertson. Sur. James
Robertson. Married by Rev. Thomas Sparks. p. 18

19 December 1796. Joseph FULLER and Susannah Aaron, dau. of
Abraham Aaron who consents. Sur. Isaac Aaron. Married by
Rev. James Tompkins. p. 22

20 October 1800. Smith FULTON and Polley Cunningham. Sur.
Joseph Norton. p. 28

15 December 1794. David FUQUA and Drucilla Terry. Sur.
Joseph Akin. Married by Rev. Lazarus Dodson. p. 18

21 November 1780. David GAMBEL and Margaret Razon. Sur.
Paul Razon. Signs her own consent. p. 3

15 December 1792. James GAMMON and Rhodey Horner. Sur.
Joseph Horner. Married by Rev. Clement Nance. p. 15

24 February 1789. John GAMMON and Mary Dixon, dau. of William
Dixon who consents. p. 11

23 April 1783. Heath GARDNER and Susannah Weldon. Married
by Rev. Lazarus Dodson. p. 5

25 January 1785. Silvany GARDNER and Elizabeth Weldon. Married by Rev. Lazarus Dodson. p. 6

30 April 1796. William GARDNER and Sally Reiger, dau. of Jacob Reiger who consents. Sur. Samuel Read. p. 22

8 August 1803. Lewis GARNER and Betsey Reiger. Sur. Jacob Reiger. Signs her own consent. p. 34

23 September 1784. Leonard GARRETT and Margaret Gover. Married by Rev. David Barr. p. 5

3 October 1803. Dudley GATEWOOD and Temperance Worsham, dau. of Robert Worsham. Sur. Robert Glasgow. p. 34

11 April 1785. Britten GEORGE and Sarah Ridel. Married by Rev. Thomas Sparks. p. 6

8 November 1794. Hugh GEORGE and Ceelia McHenry, dau. of Cornealus McHenry who consents. Sur. John Turner. p. 18

-- ---- 1803. James GILBERT and Christian Keen. Married by Rev. David Nowlin. p. 35

4 December 1801. Stephen GILES and Nancey Easley. Sur. Thomas Easley. Married by Rev. Richard Elliott. p. 31

7 January 1801. William GILES and Lucy Allen, dau. of James Allen who consents. Sur. Hartwell Allen. p. 31

18 January 1785. Robert GILMORE and Lucy Mitchell. Married by Rev. Samuel Harris. p. 6

30 September 1803. Rodham GILPIN and Martha Shaw, dau. of Thomas Shaw who consents. Sur. Robert Shaw. p. 34

12 December 1804. Abel GILTON and Elizabeth Chatmon. Sur. Thomas Worsham. p. 37

16 January 1796. James GIVENS and Molley Cottrill, dau. of William and Mary Cottrill who consent. Sur. William Cottrill. Married by Rev. Lazarus Dodson. p. 22

7 March 1788. John GIVINGS and Elizabeth Seals. Sur. John Bolling. Married by Rev. Samuel Harris. p. 10

21 November 1785. Robert GLASCOCK and Sally Shelton, dau. of Sarah Shelton who consents. Sur. Gabriel May. Married by Rev. Samuel Harris. p. 6

4 April 1803. Henry GLASS and Elizabeth Mottley, dau. of Daniel Mottly who consents. Sur. Robert Duprey. p. 34

13 December 1794. James A. GLENN and Isabella Wilson. Sur. Micajah Watkins. p. 18

24 July 1786. James GOAD and Mary Collier. Married by Rev. David Barr. p. 8

-- ---- 1789. John GOAD and Mary Gilbert. p. 11

25 September 1804. Richard GOAD and Nancy Towler, dau. of Joseph Towler who consents. Sur. Elijah Towler. p. 37

23 November 1805. Thomas GOAD and Sally Towler, dau. of Joseph Towler who consents. Sur. Elijah Towler. p. 39

17 December 1801. Robert GOODING and Susanna Brown. Married by Rev. John Atkinson. p. 31

11 November 1805. Robert GOODWIN and Rhoda Terry, dau. of Thomas Terry who consents. Sur. John Brown. Married by Rev. James Nelson. p. 39

2 April 1803. Walker GOODWIN and Susanna Musteen. Sur. Elijah Creel. Signs her own consent. p. 34

24 May 1792. John GORDON and Martha Harness. Married by Rev. Clement Nance. p. 15

20 July 1796. Joseph GOSNELL and Salley Wilkinson. Sur. Thomas Layne. p. 22

2 July 1803. Reuben GOSSETT and Elizabeth Brock. Sur. Thomas Wier. Signs her own consent. Married by Rev. James Nelson. p. 34

27 December 1791. John GOVER and Polley Dyer. Sur. Abner Dyer. Married by Rev. Richard Elliott. p. 14

6 June 1795. Samuel GOVER and Tabitha Best. Sur. Jacob Uhes - Shouldn't this be Hughes? p. 20

15 December 1800. Philip L. GRASTY and Nancey Shelton. Sur. Robertson Shelton. Crispen Shelton guardian of Nancy consents. Married by Rev. John Jenkins. p. 29

7 December 1798. William GRAVELY and Elizabeth Warren, dau. of Henry Warren who consents. Sur. Joseph Warren. Married by Rev. James Tompkins. p. 25

15 April 1793. Jeremiah GRAY and Nancy Williams, dau. of Ben Williams who consents. Sur. John Williams. p. 17

16 October 1799. Joshua GRAY and Elizabeth Elliott. Sur. Elijah Billings. Benjamin Williams signs certificate and is designated "Father". p. 26

35

2 January 1792. Thomas GREEN and Amey Keezee, dau. of Jessee Keezee who consents. Sur. Pleasant Fears. p. 15

15 January 1783. Isaac GREGGORY and Susanna Ferguson. Married by Rev. John Bailey. p. 5

7 February 1805. William GREGGORY and Polley Gannaway. Married by Rev. Griffith Dickinson. p. 39

14 December 1792. Isaac GREGORY and Milicent Ferguson. Sur. Walter Lamb. p. 15

14 January 1790. Jacob GREIDER and Mary Reither, dau. of Josonne Reither who consents. Sur. Martin Dubs, Jr. p. 12

29 September 1795. Joseph GRIFFITH and Sally Prosize. Married by Rev. Richard Elliott. p. 20

25 January 1800. William GRIFFITH and Jaley Murphy, dau. of Thomas Murphy who consents. Sur. Samuel Parsons. p. 29

20 February 1795. James GRIGGS and Ruth Goven. Sur. William Goven. p. 20

18 July 1795. John GRIGGS and Rachel Long, dau. of Edward and Janey Long who consent. Sur. Richard Elliott. Married by Rev. Richard Elliott. p. 20

21 June 1802. Wright GRIGGS and Rebekah Fallon. Sur. Redmond Fallon. p. 33

19 May 1792. Joseph GRIMES and Elizabeth Conneley. Sur. William Crane. Married by Rev. Clement Nance. p. 15

20 April 1790. Laboun GRISHAM and Martha Cunningham. Sur. Isaac Curry. Consent of Thomas and Elizabeth Grisham for Laboun. Consent of Thomas Cunningham for Martha. p. 12

20 March 1799. Joseph GRYMES and Hester Billings. Sur. Labon Graham. p. 26

21 September 1795. Samuel M. GUFFORD and Salley Elliott. Sur. George Adams. p. 20

29 August 1792. Walter GUILD and Elizabeth Conn. Sur. John Mack. p. 15

22 December 1800. David GUNN and Eleanor Sparks. Sur. Matthew W.V. Sparks. Married by Rev. Thomas Sparks. p. 29

15 December 1802. John GWIN and Winfred Bates, dau. of Samuel Bates who consents. Sur. William Bates. Married by Rev. James Nelson. p. 33

17 March 1800. Thomas GWIN and Molley Baker. Sur. William Wright. p. 29

14 February 1793. Homes GWYNE and Lucy Asten, dau. of Mary Asten who consents. Sur. Robert Asten. Married by Rev. Matthew Bates. p. 17

10 December 1793. Josiah GWYNE and Ruth Falling. Sur. Redmond Falling. p. 17

22 December 1800. Lewis HAGOOD and Edee A-ams, dau. of John Adams, Jr., who consents. Sur. Henry Hagood. Married by Rev. Richard Elliott. p. 29

24 November 1803. Ambrose HAILEY and Polly Ford, dau. of Henry Ford who consents. Sur. Jarrel Ford. p. 35

9 November 1792. Griffith HAINES and Mary Davis. Sur. Thomas Watson. Married by Rev. Richard Elliott. p. 15

13 September 1788. Ambrose HAILEY, Jr., and Nancy Ogletree. Sur. George Thompson. Signs her own consent. Married by Rev. Lazarus Dodson. p. 10

8 October 1785. George HALL and Susanna Hamblin. Sur. William Murry. Signs her own consent. Married by Rev. Lazarus Dodson. p. 6

15 January 1793. Henry HALL and Elizabeth Quinn. Sur. William Quinn. p. 17

8 December 1804. Reubin HALL and Nancy Bradley. Sur. Daniel Bradley. Married by Rev. David Nowlin. p. 37

3 September 1782. Joel HAMBLIN and Nelly Mullings. Married by Rev. James Robinson. p. 4

29 January 1796. John HAMBLIN and Sarah Harrison. Sur. Nimrod Scott. p. 22

15 August 1791. Thomas HAMES and Nancy James. Sur. Thomas Hames. Married by Rev. Matthew Bates. p. 14

2 April 1788. James HAMILTON and Amily Dove, dau. of Joseph and Mary Dove who consent. Sur. William Todd. p. 10

-- ---- 1788. Daniel HAMMOCK and Aggy Prewett. Married by Rev. Richard Elliott. p. 10

-- May 1784. John HAMMOCK and Elizabeth Gord. Married by Rev. John Bailey. p. 5

15 March 1802. Lewis HAMMOCK and Keziah Daniel. Sur. Ephraim
Hammock. p. 33

20 December 1800. William HAMMOCK and Jane Long, dau. of
Edward Long who consents. Sur. Isaac Long. p. 29

22 April 1801. John HAMPTON and Elizabeth Jenkins, dau. of
Philip Jenkins who consents. Sur. Thomas Beck. Married by
Rev. Thomas Sparks. p. 31

23 September 1784. William HAMTON and Janey Muse. Married
by Rev. Thomas Sparks. p. 5

12 February 1771. David HANBY and Jenny Dalton, dau. of Samuel
Dalton who consents. Sur. Thomas Hutchings. p. 1

24 March 1769. Jonathan HANBY and Sarah Dalton. Sur. Archeleus
Hughes. p. 1

19 December 1790. John HANKINS and Elizabeth Durham. Married
by Rev. Richard Elliott. p. 12

7 February 1800. Reubin HANKINS and Betsy Covington. Sur.
William Hawkins. Married by Rev. Clement Nance. Edmund
Covington and Betsy Covington sign certificate with no relation-
ship stated. p. 29

12 January 1796. William HANKINS and Mary Austin. Sur. David
Austin. p. 22

29 October 1791. George HANKS and Lurane Hill, dau. of Thomas
Hill who consents. Sur. Jonathan Still. Married by Rev.
John Atkinson. p. 14

23 August 1768. Adonijah HARBOUR and Ann Dalton, dau. of
Samuel Dalton who consents and is surety. p. 1

25 February 1779. William HARDAWAY, Jr., and Polley White.
Sur. Robert Williams. Consent of Jose White. p. 2

14 August 1792. Isham HARDEY and Polley Snead. Sur. Frederick
Trump. Isham Hardey son of Thomas Hardy. Samuel Snead consents
for Polley. p. 15

-- ---- 1794. John HARDEY and Anne Lewis. Married by Rev.
Thomas Sparks. p. 19

24 October 1801. Lewis HARDEY and Salley Bennett, dau. of
William Bennett who consents. Sur. Thomas Hardey. Married by
Rev. Richard Elliott. p. 31

7 December 1796. Moses HARDEY and Salley Myers. Sur. Jacob
Myers. Thomas Hardey signs certificate. Married by Rev.
Richard Elliott. p. 22

3 October 1797. James HARDIN and Mary Burgess. Sur. William Burgess. p. 24

16 September 1789. John HARDWICK and Keziah Harris. Sur. Daniel Harris. p. 11

17 May 1802. Pleasant HARDWICK and Michal Parrott. Sur. Isaac Hill. Signs her own consent. p. 33

18 July 1797. Jesse HARDY and Lightee Fitzgerald, dau. of John Fitzgerald who consents. Sur. Edmund Fitzgerald. Married by Rev. Lazarus Dodson. p. 24

-- ---- December 1783. John HARDY and Zuriah Fouster. Married by Rev. John Bailey. p. 5

20 November 1802. Reubin HARDY and Judith Bennett. Sur. Hezekiah Bennett. Signs her own consent. Married by Rev. Richard Elliott. p. 33

25 June 1790. Thomas HARDY and Keziah Powel. Sur. Seeton Beadles. Signs her own consent. Married by Rev. Richard Elliott. p. 12

17 May 1799. Thomas HARDY and Sally Craine, dau. of Susanna Craine who consents. Sur. Frederick Trumpass. Married by Rev. Richard Elliott. p. 27

25 August 1797. Hezekiah HARNESS and Elizabeth Gray. Sur. John Prescott. p. 24

21 December 1799. Thomas HARNESS and Dochia Waller. Sur. Jonas Waller. Consent of Phaney Ferguson who is designated as "Father". Married by Rev. Richard Elliott. p. 26

22 May 1793. Abednigo HARP and Elizabeth Right, dau. of Thomas and Hannah Right who consent. Sur. John Pierce. p. 17

23 January 1794. James HARP and Mary Shaw. Sur. John Watts. p. 19

13 October 1804. Nicholas HARPER and Nancy Hutcherson. Sur. Zachariah Riddle. Married by Rev. Richard Elliott. p. 37

15 December 1794. Benjamin HARRIS and Lucy Conway. Sur. William Payne. Married by Rev. Richard Elliott. p. 19

16 February 1797. James HARRIS and Seany Hackworth. Sur. William Harris. John Johnson, step-father, consents. For which one? Probably the bride. Married by Rev. Clement Nance. p. 24

4 December 1804. James HARRIS and Salley Yeatts, dau. of Stephen Yeatts who consents. Sur. Joseph M. Yeatts. Married by Rev. Willis Hopwood. p. 37

39

14 October 1793. Peter M. HARRIS and Smithey Laneford, dau. of Henry Laneford who consents. Sur. George F. Harris. p. 17

2 February 1795. Robert HARRIS and Agness Paine. Sur. Thomas Dix. p. 20

20 April 1789. Walker HARRIS and Leah Durrat. Sur. William Durrat. p. 11

10 November 1795. William HARRIS and Jaibey Gibson, dau. of James and Frances Gibson who consent. Sur. Isham Langsford. Married by Rev. Clement Nance. p. 20

15 June 1801. William HARRIS and Lucy Cheatham. Sur. Ben Harris. p. 31

16 July 1803. Andrew HARRISON and Mary Richardson, dau. of William Richardson who consents. Sur. James Richardson. p. 35

24 March 1785. Answorth HARRISON and Dolley Coleman Stone, dau. of Joshua Stone who consents. Sur. James Akin. p. 6

30 November 1784. Robert HARRISON and Anne Payne, dau. of Robert Payne who consents. Sur. Daniel Tompkins. Married by Rev. Samuel Harris. p. 5

3 October 1789. William HARRISON and Salley Hall, dau. of Jane Hall who consents. Sur. John Stanfield. p. 11

28 March 1798. William K. HARRISON and Mary H. Read, dau. of Jonathan Read who consents. Sur. John Thomas. Married by Rev. William Wright. p. 25

29 August 1794. John HARVEY and Nancy Lewis. Sur. Stephen McMillion. Samuel Lewis consents for Nancy. p. 19

12 January 1793. Samuel HARVEY and Alice Burnett. Sur. Edward Burnett. p. 17

3 September 1801. Berryman HATCHETT and Rachel Shelton. Married by Rev. Thomas Payne. p. 31

7 February 1804. Joseph HATCHETT and Elizabeth Berger, dau. of John Berger who consents. Sur. Thomas Payne. Married by Rev. Thomas Payne. p. 37

10 March 1782. Thomas HATFIELD and Mary Trigg. Married by Rev. James Robinson. p. 4

5 January 1791. Ambrose HAWKER and Cloe Murray. Sur. Bessell Hawker. p. 14

22 March 1794. Bazdel HAWKER and Polley Prewett. Married by
Rev. Richard Elliott. p. 19

16 January 1800. Joshau HAYMES and Polley Robinson. Sur.
William Haymes. Joseph Haymes father of Joshua consents. p. 29

22 December 1794. William HAYMES and Jean Dalton, dau. of
John Dalton who consents. Sur. John Thompson. Married by Rev.
Matthew Bates. p. 19

17 September 1797. Holland HEADSPETH and Mary Tate. Sur.
Nathan Tate. Married by Rev. George Dodson. p. 24

27 November 1792. Reubin HEARNDON and Hannah Long, dau. of
Edward and Pain Long who consent. Sur. Moses Long. Married
by Rev. Richard Elliott. p. 15

8 July 1802. Jacob HEDDRICK and Caty Mease, dau. of Philip
Mease who consents. Sur. Henry Headrick. p. 31

-- ---- 1800. Jacob HEDRICK and Molley Reiter. Married by
Rev. Thomas Douglas. p. 29

5 December 1798. John HEDRICK and Molley Waggoner. Married
by James Tompkins. p. 25

25 August 1781. Richard HEND and Mary Hall. Married by Rev.
John Bailey. p. 3

17 October 1781. James HENDERSON and Elizabeth Buckley. Sur.
Joseph Akin. p. 14

27 February 1792. William HENDERSON and Mary George, dau.
of James George who consents. Sur. Hugh George. p. 15

15 January 1787. Ezekial HENDRICK and Jane Hurt. Sur. Thomas
Shelton. p. 9

29 June 1787. Humphrey HENDRICK and Anna David Reynolds.
Sur. William Reynolds. p. 9

23 December 1805. John HENRY and Martha Williams. Sur. John
Williams. Married by Rev. John Atkinson. p. 39

22 February 1799. Robert HENRY and Peggy Dyer. Sur. Francis
Henry. p. 27

22 March 1786. Benjamin HENSLEY and Elenor Hampton. Married
by Rev. David Barr. p. 8

21 January 1799. Taliaferro HENSLEY and Diadamy Gorman.
Sur. David Nowlin. Signs her own consent. p. 26

12 April 1793.   James HENSON and Hannah Phillips, dau. of Tobias Phillips who consents.   Sur. John Bo-bett.   p. 17

9 November 1804.   William HERNDON and Elizabeth Long, dau. of Edward Long who consents.   Sur. William Hammock.   Married by Rev. Richard Elliott.   p. 37

16 December 1805.   William HERRING and Patsey Terry, dau. of Thomas Terry who consents.   Sur. Robert Gooding.   Married by Rev. John Atkinson.   p. 39

20 July 1799.   Samuel HESTER and Elizabeth Trahern.   Sur. Samuel Trahern.   Nehimiah Trahern consents.   p. 26

4 December 1799.   Steth (Stith?) HIGHTOWER and Rebekah Marlow, dau. of Abil Marlow who consents.   Sur. Stephen Yates.   p. 27

7 July 1787.   Charles HILL and Deborah Payne.   Sur. W. Wright. Married by Rev. Lazarus Dodson.   p. 9

7 January 1799.   Isaac HILL and Patsey B. Dix, dau. of William Dix who consents.   Sur. Joshua Grant.   Married by Rev. William Wright.   p. 27

29 October 1795.   Jonathan HILL and Ann Chaney.   Sur. George Hanks.   Married by Rev. John Atkinson.   p. 20

14 September 1785.   Joseph HILL and Sarah Wildon.   Sur. Thomas Hill.   Married by Rev. Lazarus Dodson.   p. 6 /

24 July 1804.   Joseph HILOR and Patsey Flippin, dau. of Thomas Flippin who consents.   Sur. Talliaferro Carter.   p. 37

22 December 1802.   John HINES and Lytha Lester.   Sur. Benjamin Ballinger.   John Ballinger signs certificate.   She signs her own consent as Sytha Lester.   Married by Rev. Griffith Dickinson. John Ballinger must have been her step-father as he married Lithe Lister March 1789.   p. 33

7 April 1786.   James HINTON and Lettice White.   Consent of Jesse White.   Sur. William White.   Married by Rev. Hawkins Lendrum.   p. 8

19 November 1787.   Claiborne HIX and Elizabeth Keesee.   Sur. Charles Keesee.   p. 9

18 April 1785.   Samuel HOBSON and Elizabeth Lewis, dau. of John Lewis who consents.   Sur. Robert Lewis.   p. 6

16 April 1792.   Charles HODGES and Levency Gilbert.   Sur. Preston Gilbert.   p. 15

12 December 1795.   David HODGES and Elizabeth Hubbard.   Sur. Joseph Akin.   p. 20

20 March 1805. Daniel HODNETT and Elizabeth Bryant. Sur. Elisha Bryant. Married by Rev. Richard Elliott. p. 39

9 November 1792. John HODNETT and Lucy Davis. Sur. Ralph Dodson. Signs her own consent. Married by Rev. Lazarus Dodson. p. 15

28 May 1782. John HOLDER and Elizabeth Jennings. Married by Rev. John Bailey. p. 4

21 November 1792. John HOLDER and Martha Caldwell. Sur. William Jones. Married by Rev. Matthew Bates. p. 15

2 February 1803. John HOLDER and Milley Holder. Sur. Spencer Holder. Married by Rev. Griffith Dickinson. p. 35

22 June 1803. Spencer HOLDER and Molley Holder. Sur. John Holder. Married by Rev. Thomas Payne. p. 35

4 May 1795. Michael HOLLAND and Agnes Ward. Sur. Jeremiah Ward. Married by Rev. Thomas Douglas. p. 20

1 November 1802. Leonard HOLLEY and Betsy Dalton. Sur. George Dalton. p. 33

17 December 1804. William HOLLIGAN and Elizabeth Bargerly. Sur. John Bargerly. Married by Rev. Thomas Sparks. p. 37

21 December 1801. Anthony HOLLOWAY and Nancy Williams. Sur. W. Wright. p. 31

13 April 1798. Edmond HOLLOWAY and Nancey Hedspeth. Sur. James Collie. James Holloway father of Edmond. Nancy signs her own consent. p. 25

16 February 1799. John HOLLOWAY and Susanna Fitzgerald, dau. of John Fitzgerald who consents. Sur. Edmond Holloway. p. 27

24 November 1803. Joseph HOLT and Ann S. McDaniel. Married by Rev. Griffith Dickinson. p. 35

23 January 1801. Miles HOLT and Salley Fowlkes, dau. of James Fowlkes who consents and is surety. p. 31

23 October 1793. James HOPKINS and Frances Carter, dau. of Jesse Carter who consents. Sur. Joseph Akin. p. 17

15 November 1797. James HOPKINS and Mary Carter, dau. of Jesse Carter who consents. Sur. George Wright. p. 24

15 November 1798. John HOPWOOD and Nancey Huffman. Sur. Jacob Huffman. Berbery Huffman consents for Nancey. p. 25

7 July 1800. Willis HOPWOOD and Penelope Moore, dau. of Thomas Moore who consents. Sur. John Hopwood. p. 29

2 August 1785. John HOSKINS and Elizabeth Lovell. Sur. Daniel Lovell. p. 6

13 November 1800. Johnson HOSKINS and Rebecca Johnson. Sur. Dudley Farthing. Signs her own consent. Married by Rev. Richard Elliott. p. 29

14 December 1801. William HOSKINS and Nancy Willis. Sur. Langston Johnson. Thomas Hoskins father of William. Married by Rev. Thomas Payne. p. 31

20 October 1794. Isham HUBBARD and Sarah Brown. Sur. Joseph Akin. Married by Rev. Richard Elliott. p. 19

30 December 1798. Moses HUBBARD and Elizabeth Hodges, dau. of John Hodges who consents and is surety. Married by Rev. James Tompkins. p. 25

12 September 1787. Reubin HUBBARD and Sarah Morgan. Sur. James Templeton. Signs her own consent. p. 9

-- ---- 1800. Reubin HUBBARD and Elizabeth Cockram. Married by Rev. John Jenkins. p. 29

7 August 1802. Samuel HUBBARD and Obedience Alexander, dau. of William Alexander who consents. Sur. William Wright. p. 33

19 July 1802. Robert HUCY and Polley Fuller. Sur. W. Wright. Married by Rev. Thomas Payne. p. 33

1 December 1790. John HUDDLESTON and Mourning Thompson. Sur. Joseph Thompson. Married by Rev. John Atkinson. p. 12

4 September 1802. Jeremiah HUDSON and Mille Bucey. Sur. Edward Bucey. p. 33

-- ---- 1800. Thomas HUDSON and Nancy Denton. Married by Rev. Thomas Douglas. p. 29

20 August 1769. Archeleus HUGHES and Mary Dalton, dau. of Samuel Dalton who consents. Sur. Will Tunstall. p. 1

17 January 1803. James HUGHES and Susanna Reynolds. Sur. George Reynolds. Married by Rev. Clement Nance. p. 35

21 November 1796. Richard HUGHES and Bettsey Reynolds, dau. of George and Susanna Reynolds who consent. Sur. John Morehead. Married by Rev. Clement Nance. p. 22

13 June 1782. Robert HUGHEY and Leweasia Thompson. Married by Rev. John Bailey. Shouldn't this be Louisa? p. 4

25 July 1804. Philip HUKER and Sally Snody, dau. of John Snody who consents. Sur. William Snody. p. 37

6 February 1778. Caleb HUNDLEY and Sarah Walker, dau. of Joseph Walker who consents. Sur. James Mitchell. p. 2

21 July 1788. John HUNDLEY and Mary Jones. Sur. Joseph Terry. Signs her own consent. p. 10

8 October 1801. John HUNDLEY and Dorcas Sanders, dau. of William Sanders who consents. Sur. David Parker. p. 31

17 May 1790. Dandridge HURT and Lucy Shelton, dau. of John Shelton who consents. Sur. Vincent Shelton. Married by Rev. Lazarus Dodson. p. 12

25 September 1789. Garland HURT and Mertisha Thurston, dau. of John Thurston who consents. Sur. Thomas Shelton. p. 11

16 January 1804. Robert HURT and Polley W. Williams. Sur. James M. Williams. Married by Rev. John Atkinson. p. 37

14 January 1799. John HUTCHERSON and Jency Linthicum, dau. of Thomas Linthicum who consents. Sur. John Giles, Jr. Married by Rev. James Tompkins. p. 27

13 June 1784. Walter HUTCHERSON and Mary Payne. Married by Rev. John Bailey. p. 5

18 August 1788. James HUTCHINGS and Martha Parks. Sur. John Parks. p. 10

13 December 1780. Moses HUTCHINGS and ---- ---- Parks. Sur. Joseph Akin. p. 3

29 August 1785. Thomas HUTCHINGS and Tallitha Blackgrove, dau. of Henry Blackgrove who consents. Sur. Aaron Hutchings. Married by Rev. David Barr. p. 6

18 January 1804. John HUTCHISON and Susanna Burton, dau. of Elisha Burton who consents. Sur. William Burton. Married by Rev. Richard Elliott. p. 37

5 November 1804. Thomas HUTCHISON and Nancy Burgess. Sur. Hardin Burgess. Married by Rev. Richard Elliott. p 37

3 April 1786. John Peter HUTSON and Joice Fearns, dau. of Arthur Fearns who consents. Sur. James Turley. Married by Rev. David Barr. p. 8

1 November 1792. Thomas HUTSON and Nancy Denton. Sur. Thomas
Denton. p. 15

15 February 1796. Garland INGRAM and Hannah Maize. Sur.
William Ingram. Signs her own consent. p. 22

11 March 1799. Larkin INGRAM and Caty Humphrey. Sur. William
Davis. Married by Rev. John Atkinson. p. 27

15 July 1799. Tarpley INGRAM and Mourning Mayse. Sur. Thomas
Mayse. Married by Rev. George Dodson. p. 27

28 December 1803. Edmund INMAN and Fanny Thurman. Sur. William
Thurman. Married by Rev. David Nowlin. p. 35

20 June 1803. Henry INMAN and Lydea Anglin. Sur. Daniel
Boaz. Married by Rev. Richard Elliott. p. 35

26 March 1804. Jesse INMAN and Clara Foster. Sur. James
Foster. Married by Rev. Richard Elliott. p. 37

16 December 1805. Shandrack INMAN and Nancy Ramsey. Sur.
Henry Inman who also signs certificate. Married by Rev. William
Blair. p. 39

18 December 1792. Edmund IRBY and Rebeccah Williams. Married
by Rev. Lazarus Dodson. p. 15

-- ---- 1799. Francis IRBY and Patsy Glenn. Married by Rev.
John Jenkins. p. 27

15 December 1797. Samuel IRBY and Milley Davis. Married by
Rev. Thomas Payne. p. 24

3 March 1795. William IRBY and Anne Farmer. Married by Rev.
John Jenkins. p. 20

19 June 1787. John JAMES and Dinnah Haynes. Sur. William
Haynes. p. 9

21 July 1789. John T. JAMES and Rachel Streetman. Sur. John
Gammon. Signs her own consent. p. 11

27 July 1792. John JAMES and Elizabeth Guthrey. Sur. Nathan
Cunningham. Married by Rev. Lazarus Dodson. p. 15

27 October 1803. William JAMES and Charity Jolley. Sur.
Francis Shaw. p. 35

3 January 1798. Archibald JEFFERSON and Levina Ramsey, dau.
of Thomas and Frances Ramsey who consent. Sur. Thomas Ramsey.
p. 25

46

12 October 1800. John JEFFERSON and Anna Ramsey, dau. of Frances Ramsey who consents. Sur. Noton Ramsey. p. 29

23 April 1780. William JENKINS and Samoras Roberts, dau. of James Roberts who consents. Sur. Henry Coneay. p. 3

2 February 1797. John JENNINGS and Peggy Collie. Married by Rev. Richard Elliot. p. 24

6 May 1785. Daniel JETT and Salley Smith. Sur. Peyton Smith. Married by Rev. David Barr. p. 6

21 September 1801. A-raham JOHNS and Patsey Austin. Sur. Joseph Johns. p. 31

12 November 1804. William JOHNS and Elizabeth L. Hillard. Married by Rev. Griffith Dickinson. p. 37

28 September 1803. Arthur JOHNSON and Nancy Fielder. Sur. Samuel Parsons. Signs her own consent. Married by Rev. Richard Elliott. p. 35

18 April 1805. James JOHNSON and Nancy Woodson, dau. of Allen Woodson who consents. Sur. Joseph Yates. Married by Rev. David Nowlin. p. 39

26 September 1796. Langston JOHNSON and Polley Jones, dau. of William Jones who consents. Sur. William Sheppard. p. 22

30 December 1800. Obediah JOHNSON and Rossey Prewet. Sur. Elijah Prewet. Married by Rev. Richard Elliott. p. 29

3 November 1785. Philip JOHNSON and Susanna Payne. Married by Rev. David Barr. p. 6

15 March 1795. Richard JOHNSON and Lettice Hinson. Sur. Jere White. Signs her own consent. Married by Rev. Lazarus Dodson who says Hinton. p. 20

17 January 1795. Thomas JOHNSON and Mary Robinson. Sur. Nicholas Robinson. p. 21

26 June 1777. Samuel JOHNSTON and Elizabeth Ballinger, dau. of Joseph Ballinger who consents. Sur. James Akin. p. 2

27 July 1793. Buckner JONES and Nelly Wilson. Sur. Travis Lee. p. 17

1 December 1792. Dudley JONES and Nancy Ellington, dau. of Jeremiah Ellington who consents. Sur. John Waldron. p. 15

1 December 1799. Emanuel JONES and Martha Smith. Sur. John B. Dawson. Signs her own consent. p. 27

14 April 1799. Lewis JONES and Fanny Lamb. Sur. Richard Mitchell. Signs her own consent. Married by Rev. Clement Nance. p. 27

13 February 1804. Sanford JONES and Mary Hodges, dau. of John Hodges who consents and is surety. Married by Rev. John King. p. 37

24 August 1803. Edward JORDAN and Polley Barnett, dau. of Thomas Barnett who consents. Sur. Joseph Barnett. p. 35

5 September 1803. George JUSTICE and Nancy Smith. Sur. Samuel Smith. Married by Rev. David Nowlin. p. 35

15 February 1798. John JUSTICE and Elizabeth Young, dau. of Archibald and Sarah Young who consent. Sur. Robert Powell. Married by Rev. Thomas Douglas. p. 25

28 July 1785. Philip KEARBY and Jeriah Potter. Married by Rev. David Barr. p. 6

11 March 1779. Charles KEATTS and Archer Clark. Sur. Thomas Weller. Signs her own consent. p. 2

19 November 1792. Richard KEATTS and Elizabeth Waller, dau. of John Waller who consents. Sur. Fred Shelton. Married by Rev. Matthew Bates. p. 15

25 July 1801. Thomas KEATTS and Nancy R. Williams. Sur. William Williams. Married by Rev. Thomas Payne. p. 31

21 November 1305. Benjamin KEESEE and Milley Arthur, dau. of Joseph Arthur who consents. Sur. David Parker. p. 39

15 August 1803. Richard KEESEE and Jenney McMurry. Sur. Francis McClanahan. Married by Rev. Thomas Payne. p. 35

28 November 1794. James KEEZEE and Elizabeth White, dau. of Benjamin and Ginny White who consent. Sur. John Piercy. p. 19

4 September 1793. Jeremiah KEEZEE and Dorchas Perkins. Sur. Robert Martin. Shouldn't this be Dorcas? p. 17

19 March 1788. John KEEZEE and Betsey Parsons. Sur. George Parsons. Married by Rev. Samuel Harris. p. 10

26 April 1787. Hugh KELLEY and Jinsy Haring. Married by Rev. James Hinton. p. 9

1 April 1780. John KENDRICK and Ann Neal. Sur. Joseph Akin. p. 3

28 January 1782. John KENDRICK and Ann Neal. Signs her own consent. p. 4

48

22 February 1799. Ozburn KENDRICK and Polley Phillips, dau. of James Phillips who consents. Sur. William Watkins. Married by Rev. George Dodson. p. 27

25 November 1803. John KERBY and Anne Brown, dau. of Frederick Brown who consents. Sur. Langston Brown. Married by Rev. Thomas Payne. p. 35

20 December 1790. Richard KERBY and Elenor Kerby. Sur. Jacob Kerby. Consent of John Kerby (for which one?). p. 12

22 November 1797. Richard KIGGINS and Winifred Pistole. Married by Rev. Lazarus Dodson. p. 24

23 August 1770. Edmund KING and Mary Thomas. Sur. Francis Luck. Signs her own consent. p. 1

5 March 1801. Elijah KING and Tabitha Terry. Married by Rev. Elias Dodson. p. 31

10 August 1796. John KING and Anna Terry, dau. of Henry and Mary Terry who consent. Sur. Francis Shaw. Married by Rev. Lazarus Dodson. p. 22

7 February 1799. Royall KING and Milley Corbin. Sur. Randolph Corbin. p. 27

6 October 1780. Tobias KINGARY and Mary Aaron, dau. of Abraham Aaron who consents. Sur. Joseph Akin. p. 3

13 December 1789. Boling KIRBY and Milley Campbell, dau. of Abraham Campbell who consents. Consent of John Kerby for Boling. Sur. Joel Thacker. p. 11

25 November 1801. John LACY and Betsey Griffey. Sur. William Griffey. p. 31

17 July 1797. Sharp LAMKIN and Polly Wimbish, dau. of John Wimbish who consents. Sur. John Wimbish, Jr. p. 24

23 December 1790. David LAW and Avey Willis. Sur. Joel Willis. Married by Rev. Lazarus Dodson. p. 13

24 November 1789. Bird LAWLESS and Susanna Thomas. Married by Rev. Richard Elliott. p. 11

25 December 1786. John LAWLESS and Sarah Tanner. Sur. W. Wright. Married by Rev. Lazarus Dodson. p. 8

2 September 1788. John LAWRENCE and Beheathaland Smith, dau. of George Smith who consents. Sur. Joseph Akin. Married by Rev. Thomas Douglas. p. 10

5 May 1785. William LAWRENCE and Rachel Fuller. Sur. Samuel Callana. Married by Rev. Samuel Harris? p. 6

18 June 1804. Rowland LAWSON and Patsey Durrett. Sur. Francis Durrett. Signs her own consent. p. 37

2 July 1799. Bartlet LAY and Elenor Robinson. Sur. James Robinson. p. 27

16 June 1795. David LAYNE and Mary Wilson. Sur. William T. Galden. p. 21

9 July 1804. Hilary LAYNE and Sally Wilson, dau. of George Wilson who consents. Sur. John Jones. Married by Rev. William Davis. p. 37

18 July 1790. Moses LAYNE and Frances Oliver. Married by Rev. Richard Elliott. p. 13

13 March 1790. Thomas LAYNE and Elizabeth Wilkinson. Sur. Nathan Brown. Signs her own consent. p. 13

-- ---- 1803. Jesse LEFTWICH and Sally Briscoe. Married by Rev. Thomas Sparks. p. 35

-- December 1784. Abraham LEGRAND and Lucy Owen. Married by Rev. Samuel Harris. p. 5

20 November 1797. George LEGRAND and Nancy Elliott, dau. of Jonathan Elliott who consents. Sur. Samuel McGufford. p. 24

16 August 1796. Samuel LEPRAD and Jane Campbell. Sur. Francis Henry. Signs her own consent. p. 22

16 March 1795. Daniel LESTER and Milly Flowers, dau. of Edward Flowers who consents. Married by Rev. John Jenkins. p. 21

-- ---- 1800. John LESTER and Nancy Collins. Married by Rev. John Jenkins. p. 29

20 November 1778. William LETCHER and Elizabeth Perkins. Sur. John Dickerson. p. 2

16 November 1799. Charles LEWIS and Gartherhood Johns. Sur. Philip Thomas. Signs her own consent. Married by Rev. Richard Elliott. p. 27

10 November 1792. George LEWIS and Sarah Hardey. Married by Rev. Lazarus Dodson. p. 15

26 September 1792. John LEWIS and Milley Shelton. Married by Rev. Thomas Payne. p. 15

26 April 1803. John LEWIS and Polley Hardey. Sur. Reubin
Lewis. George Hardey consents for Polley. Married by Rev.
Elias Dodson. p. 35

26 September 1797. Reubin LEWIS and Nancy Hardey, dau. of
George Hardey who consents. Sur. John Hardy. Married by Rev.
Lazarus Dodson. p. 24

6 April 1801. William LEWIS and Peggy H. Read. Sur. Lewis
B. Allen. Jane Read guardian of Peggy consents. p. 31

-- ---- 1793. William LINDSAY and Elizabeth Adams. Married
by Rev. Matthew Bates. p. 17

15 March 1805. Christopher LINDSEY and Sarah Adams. Sur.
John Adams. Married by Rev. David Nowlin. p. 39

13 September 1787. John LINSEY and Anna Witcher, dau. of
John Witcher who consents. Sur. Jesse Atkins. Married by Rev.
Thomas Douglas. p. 9

12 October 1791. Royal N. LIPFORD and Obedience Ellington,
dau. of S.J. Ellington who consents. Sur. Anthony Lipford.
Married by Rev. Richard Elliott. p. 14

20 August 1792. David LOGAN and Martha Snead. Sur. William
Thorp. Married by Rev. Lazarus Dodson. p. 15

10 December 1799. Charles LONG and Sarah Earp. Sur. Nicholas
Earp. p. 27

-- ---- 1804. Edward LONG and Mildred Bolton. Married by
Rev. David Nowlin. p. 37

9 June 1791. George LONG and Elizabeth Maples. Married by
Rev. Richard Elliott. p. 14

21 October 1804. Levi LONG and Susanna Elliott. Sur. Thomas
Elliott. Married by Rev. Richard Elliott. p. 37

10 October 1782. William LONG and Rachel Pruet. Married by
Rev. James Robinson. p. 4

19 January 1802. James LOVELACE and Polley Mitchell. Sur.
William G. Mitchell. James Mitchell signs certificate. p. 33

-- ---- 1799. Thomas LOVELACE and Ann Mitchell. Married by
Rev. John Jenkins. p. 27

3 May 1796. Daniel LOVELL and Susannah Watson. Sur. Levy
Watson. p. 22

17 September 1796. John LOVELL and Sarah Williams (widow). Sur. William Watson. Signs her own consent. Married by Rev. John Jenkins. p. 22

14 April 1774. William LOVELL and Mary Dudley. Sur. Daniel Lovell. Signs her own consent. p. 1

2 August 1787. Isaac LOWE and Mary Aney Browden. Sur. William Harrison. p. 9

1 May 1783. Charles LUASS and Mariah Waller. Married by Rev. Lazarud Dodson. The groom's name is indexed as Lucas. p. 5

LUCAS: See Luass

20 December 1784. John LUCK and Polley Adams. Sur. Joseph Luck. p. 5

5 September 1792. Harrison LUMKINS and Rhodey Ferguson, dau. of Joseph Ferguson who consents. Sur. Thomas Worsham. p. 15

6 May 1792. John LUMKINS and Sarah Lumkins. Married by Rev. Lazarus Dodson. p. 15

28 January 1782. George LUMPKIN and Ann Rutledge. Sur. Robert Crockett. p. 4

2 January 1800. George LUMPKIN and Nancy Smith. Sur. William Barnett. p. 29

24 December 1795. John LUMPKINS and Betsey Dix. Sur. John Fenley. Larkin and Gency Dix consent for Betsey. p. 21

21 January 1793. Joseph LYNCH and Elizabeth Crane. Sur. Josiah Short. Married by Rev. Richard Elliott. p. 17

7 February 1794. Philips MABERRY and Elizabeth Chaney. Married by Rev. Lazarus Dodson. p. 19

20 February 1797. Cornelius MABRY and Polley Chaney, dau. of Ezekel Chaney who consents. Sur. William Chaney. Married by Rev. John Atkinson. p. 24

6 December 1799. Robe-t S. MABRY and Rebekah Adams, dau. of Nathan Adams, Sr., who consents. Sur. James Welch. Married by Rev. Richard Elliott. p. 27

26 June 1790. Alexander MACHAM and Catharine Ball, dau. of John Ball who consents. Sur. George Robinson. p. 13

15 October 1805. Constantine MACK and Nancy Brunett, dau. of Gilbert Burnett who consents. Sur. John Mack, Sr. Married by Rev. William Blair. p. 39

3 February 1799. John MACK and Polly Garner, dau. of William
Garner who consents. Sur. George Hankins. p. 27

2 October 1799. William MACK and Mary Blair. Sur. George
Blair. p. 27

11 February 1800. Alexander MACKAY and Jemma Arthur, dau. of
William Arthur who consents. Sur. Jechonias Arthur. p. 29

21 December 1801. John MADDING and Polley Brooks, dau. of
Samuel Brooks, Sr., who consents. Sur. John Bingham. p. 31

28 January 1798. Thomas MADDING and Mary Dodson, dau. of
George Dodson who consents. Sur. John Madding. Married by
Rev. Lazarus Dodson. p. 25

8 October 1787. Ambrose MADDISON and Anne Lankford. Sur.
Thomas Lankford. p. 9

-- ---- 1800. Alexander MAHAN and Katherine Ball. Married
by Rev. Thomas Douglas. p. 29

2 March 1795. James MAHAN and Mary Nowlin. Sur. Joseph Devin.
Bryan Ward Nowlin consents for Mary. Married by Rev. Richard
Elliott. p. 21

26 March 1805. Samuel MAHUE and Tinah Groff, dau. of Samuel
Groff who consents. Sur. William Tunstall. Married by Rev.
Griffith Dickinson. p. 39

2 January 1792. James MALICOTT and Rhoda Witcher, dau. of
John Witcher. Married by Rev. Thomas Douglas. Sur. John
Linsey. p. 15

19 August 1794. John MALICOTT and Mary Nash, dau. of John
Nash who consents and is surety. Married by Rev. Matthew
Bates. p. 19

16 December 1805. William MALLICOAT and Elizabeth Love. Sur.
James Love. Married by Rev. Willis Hopwood. p. 39

29 January 1799. Edmond MALLICOTT and Levina Thacker, dau.
of Peter Thacker who consents and is surety. p. 27

9 November 1802. Joel MANN and Patsey Walker. Sur. Larkin
Madding. Samuel Walker signs certificate. p. 33

2 May 1797. Edward MARLOW and Rebecca Irby. Sur. Kinzee
Marlow. p. 24

13 January 1791. Kinsey MARLOW and Pinnah Keezee. Married by
Rev. Richard Elliott. p. 14

30 October 1787. Joseph MARR and Elizabeth Harnes, consent of John Kerby (for which one?). Sur. Jacob Kerby. Married by Rev. Samuel Harris. p. 9

22 March 1802. Joseph MART and Sandal Vadin. Sur. Wilson Vaden. p. 33

25 December 1795. Benjamin MARTIN and Salley Ragland. Sur. Thomas Shelton. p. 21

7 January 1802. Benjamin MARTIN and Salley Terry, dau. of Barton and Susannah Terry who consent. Sur. David Terry. Married by Rev. Elias Dodson. p. 31

15 December 1789. Isham MARTIN and Susanna Covington. Sur. Joseph Wright and Robert Martin. Signs her own consent. p. 11

-- ---- 1802. James MARTIN and Nancy Ferguson, dau. of Alexander and Marget Farguson who consent. Sur. Evins Echols. Married by Rev. Richard Elliott. p. 33

1 April 1782. John MARTIN and Susannah Jaetz. Married by Rev. John Bailey. p. 4

-- March 1797. Joseph MARTIN and Molley Hubbard. Married by Rev. James Kinney. p. 24

4 May 1789. Robert MARTIN and Tabitha Keezee. Married by Rev. Richard Elliott. p. 11

17 December 1793. Thomas MARTIN and Levicy Cundiff. Sur. Leonard Dove. Married by Rev. Matthew Bates who says Lucy. p. 17

13 November 1794. William MARTIN and Sarah Ballinger. Sur. Benjamin Ballinger. Married by Rev. James Kinney. p. 19

16 January 1805. William MARTIN and Polley Bayes, dau. of Lavasey Bayes who consents. Sur. Abraham Shelton. Married by Rev. David Nowlin. p. 39

4 November 1805. Benjamin MATHERLY and Polley Maurice. Sur. Samuel Maurice. Married by Rev. William Blair. p. 39

18 December 1800. Levi MATHERLY and Fanney Wiggenton, dau. of John Wiggenton who consents. Sur. Joseph Matherly. p. 29

22 September 1803. Samuel MATHERLY and Judith Reynolds, dau. of Jesse Reynolds who consents and is surety. Married by Rev. James Nelson. p. 35

29 December 1804. Luke MATTHEWS and Bucy Dunn. Sur. John Dunn, Jr. Married by Rev. Richard Elliott. p. 37

54

15 November 1777. John MAY and Susanna Porter. Sur. Joseph
Porter. Signs her own consent. p. 2

MAYHEW: See Mahue

6 October 1790. William MAYPOLES and Nancy Long. Married by
Rev. Richard Elliott. p. 13

-- ---- 1789. Bingham MAYS and Elizabeth Snider. p. 11

20 December 1802. Fleming MAYS and Rhoda Barber. Sur. Avery
Mustain. Married by Rev. Griffith Dickinson. p. 33

13 December 1788. Larkin MAYS and Susannah Saunders. Married
by Rev. Lazarus Dodson. p. 10

11 December 1802. Mattox MAYS and Uphan Roberts (widow).
Sur. John Robert. Eufan Roberts signs certificate. Married
by Rev. Griffith Dickinson. p. 33

19 October 1798. Thomas MAYS and Leety Ingram, dau. of William
Ingram who consents. Sur. George Dodson. Married by Rev.
Lazarus Dodson. p. 25

1 November 1781. Thomas MEADE and Sarah Davis. Sur. Benjamin
Davis. Signs her own consent. p. 3

31 July 1801. Casper MEAS and Patsey Powell. Sur. Philip
Meas. Married by Rev. John Wyatt. p. 31

17 August 1795. Spencer MEDCALF and Anne Doss. Sur. John
Doss. Married by Rev. Thomas Payne. p. 21

16 December 1796. Abraham MEDKIFF and Eythe Dalton. Sur.
John Neal. p. 22

30 October 1801. James MEDKIFF and Sally Donelson. Sur.
James Donelson. Married by Rev. Elias Dodson. p. 31

1 December 1797. Philip MEESE and Mary Powell. Sur. Robert
Powell. Married by Rev. Thomas Douglas. p. 24

11 April 1791. William MEIRS and Anne Corbin. Sur. Benjamin
Davis. Brown Corbin consents for Anne. Married by Rev.
Richard Elliott. p. 14

17 July 1792. Nathaniel MELTON and Nancy Pears. Sur. Leon
Garrett. Married by Rev. Clement Nance. p. 15

19 August 1799. Richard MELTON and Judith Earls. Sur. John
Carter. Signs her own consent. Married by Rev. Clement Nance.
p. 27

19 July 1802.   John Clark MERWIN and Jane S. Mabry.   Sur. James
T. Johnson.   Signs her own consent.   p. 33

17 October 1791.   Robert MICKELBUROUGH and Elizabeth Southerland.
Sur. Jacob Kirby.   George Southerland consents for Elizabeth.
p. 14

10 September 1782.   John MIDKIFF and Mary Parsons.   Married
by Rev. John Bailey.   p. 4

14 June 1793.   Joseph MIDKIFF and Rebecca Turley.   Sur. Joseph
Polley.   p. 17

17 November 1800.   Samuel MIDKIFF and Lydia Parsons, dau. of
John and Mary Parsons who consent.   Sur. Jesse Parsons.
Married by Rev. Thomas Payne.   p. 29

21 February 1801.   Spencer MIDKIFF and Rebekah Rigney.   Sur.
Samuel Parsons.   Married by Rev. Richard Elliott.   p. 31

-- ---- 1800.   Henry MILIRONS and Caty Barger.   Married by
Rev. Thomas Douglas.   p. 29

5 July 1794.   John MILLS and Betsy Bayes, dau. of Louise Bayes
who consents.   Sur. John Bayes.   Married by Rev. Matthew Bates.
p. 19

11 February 1790.   Daniel MITCHELL and Sarah Bradley.   Married
by Rev. Richard Elliott.   p. 13

18 November 1799.   Frederick MITCHELL and Patsey Perkins,
dau. of Mary Perkins who consents.   Sur. William Cobler.
Married by Rev. Clement Nance.   p. 27

7 December 1801.   Isaac MITCHELL and Anna Perkins, dau. of
Mary Perkins who consents.   Sur. John Ballington.   Married by
Rev. Clement Nance.   p. 31

25 November 1768.   James MITCHELL and Agitha Dalton, dau. of
Robert Dalton who consents and is surety.   p. 1

28 ---- 1779.   James MITCHELL and Sarah Waren Hubbard.   Sur.
Joseph Akin.   Signs her own consent.   p. 2

29 September 1790.   James MITCHELL and Winifred Lockett.
Sur. John Pemberton.   p. 13

15 October 1804.   John MITCHELL and Anne Atkins.   Sur. Edward
Akins.   p. 37

15 February 1794.   Rich MITCHELL and Susanna Richardson.   Sur.
George Mitchell.   Married by Rev. Thomas Sparks.   p. 19

13 August 1801. William MOODY and Betsey Dixon. Married by
Rev. Clemsnt Nance. p. 31

11 December 1800. James MOORE and Nancy Cammeron. Sur. William
Farthing. Signs her own consent. Married by Rev. Richard
Elliott. p. 29

7 January 1803. James MOORE and Elizabeth Shelhorse. Sur.
John Robertson. Married by Rev. Griffith Dickinson. p. 35

27 November 1795. James MORE and Elizabeth F. Patrick, dau.
of John Patrick who consents. Sur. Edward Patrick. p. 21

25 January 1802. Joseph MOREHEAD and Jane S. Jenkins, dau.
of Philip Jenkins who consent. Sur. David Rice. p. 33

19 November 1795. James MOREMAN and Polley Early, dau. of
Joshuway Early who consents. Sur. John Leftwitch. p. 21

23 December 1802. Hanes MORGAN and Elizabeth Shelton. Married
by Rev. Griffith Dickinson. p. 33

21 January 1800. Lewis MORGAN and Frances White, dau. of
Lucy White who consents. Sur. William Johnson. p. 29

16 November 1799. William MORRICE and Sally Stoe. Sur. James
Morrice. p. 27

12 June 1792. Samuel MORRIS and Vicey Chaney. Sur. James
Donilson. Married by Rev. Lazarus Dodson. p. 16

29 March 1805. William Morris and Nancy Inman. Sur. Jesse
Inman. Married by Rev. David Nowlin. p. 39

23 March 1804. Benjamin MORRISON and Nancey Barnes. Sur.
Josiah Barnes. p. 37

27 September 1777. John MORTON and Lucy Blackley, dau. of
James Blackley who consents. Sur. James Akin. p. 2

6 May 1778. Joseph MORTON and Chaney Harrison. Sur. Lewis
Gwilmin. Signs her own consent. p. 2

18 March 1805. Joseph MORTON and Cecelia M. Morton. Sur.
William Tunstall. Married by Rev. Thomas Sparks. p. 39

21 June 1802. Quinn MORTON and Elizabeth Sutherlin, dau. of
John Sutherlin who consents. Sur. Nath. W. Williams. p. 33

17 August 1785. David MOTLEY and Elizabeth Pendleton. Married
by Rev. David Barr. p. 6

-- ---- 1789. John MOTTLEY and Elizabeth Depea. Married by Rev. Lazarus Dodson. p. 11

9 November 1804. Joseph MOTTLEY and Salley Tanner, dau. of Creed Tanner who consents and is surety. Married by Rev. Richard Elliott. p. 37

25 November 1789. Samuel MOTTLEY and Elizabeth Terry. Married by Rev. Lazarus Dodson. p. 11

1 February 1787. Dan MULLENS and Susannah Mallicoat. Married by Rev. David Barr. p. 9

-- ---- 1785. John MULLINS and Nancy Hubbard. Married by Rev. Nathaniel Thurman. p. 6

6 December 1800. Joseph MULLINS and Nancey Hudson, dau. of John and Mary Hudson who consent. Sur. Joseph Hudson. Married by Rev. John Wyatt. p. 29

27 September 1800. Joshua MULLINS and Peggy Thomas. Sur. John Prewet. p. 29

17 August 1801. Thomas MULLINS and Prudence Cox. Sur. William Hooligan. Signs her own consent. p. 31

18 April 1803. William MULLINS and Freelove Robinson. Sur. Joseph Midkiff. Signs her own consent. Married by Rev. Richard Elliott. p. 35

5 November 1798. Jeremiah MUNDAY and Chloe Shelton, dau. of Spencer Shelton. Sur. Willis Shelton. Married by Rev. Thomas Payne. p. 25

27 March 1794. George MURPHEY and Frances Jefferson. Married by Rev. Richard Elliott. p. 19

12 February 1799. Ezikiel MURPHY and Martha Smith, dau. of Martha Smith who consents. Sur. John Smith. p. 27

25 December 1793. Thomas MURPHY and Anne Davis, dau. of John Davis who consents. Sur. James Davis. p. 17

30 July 1800. Thomas MURPHY and Rebeckah Thacker. Sur. Reubin Thacker. Married by Rev. Richard Elliott. p. 29

7 March 1786. William MURPHY and Abbe Cahill. Married by Rev. David Barr. p. 8

18 November 1805. Joel MUSE and Fanny Swanson, dau. of William Swanson, Sr., who consents. Sur. Samuel Muse. Married by Rev. Joseph Hatchett. p. 39

17 January 1803. Samuel A. MUSE and Dorothy Swanson, dau. of William Swanson who consents. Sur. James Welch. p. 35

16 April 1782. Harrison MUSGROVE and Jeane Owen. Sur. John Briscoe. p. 4

30 April 1782. Abraham MUSICK and Elizabeth Cooley. Married by Rev. Samuel Harris. p. 4

11 June 1793. Jesse MUSTAIN and Polley Brewis, dau. of Robert Brewis who consents. Sur. Leonard Dove. Married by Rev. Thomas Payne. p. 17

15 October 1804. Stephen MYERS and Dice Price. Sur. Fontaine Price. Married by Rev. Richard Elliott. p. 37

10 May 1793. James McAKRON and Peggy O'Daniel. Sur. William Burton. Signs her own consent. Married by Rev. Clement Nance. p. 17

26 September 1791. John McCOON and Agness Jennings. Married by Rev. Clement Nance. p. 14

17 November 1782. William McCRAW and Susanna Walker. Sur. Joseph Akin. p. 4

8 June 1802. John McCRICKETT and Sarah McMurray. Sur. Francis McClannahan. Married by Rev. Thomas Payne. p. 33

19 October 1779. Clement McDANIEL and Elizabeth Coleman. Sur. Stephen Coleman. p. 2

19 September 1796. Joel McDANIEL and Pattsy Price, dau. of William Price who consents. Sur. D. Coleman. p. 22

6 January 1805. Stephen C. McDANIEL and Locky Douglas. Married by Rev. Griffith Dickinson. p. 39

7 May 1797. William McDANIEL and Molley Price, dau. of William Price who consents. Sur. Joel McDaniel. p. 24

26 March 1803. Jeremiah McDONALD and Polley Harris, dau. of George F. Harris who consents. Sur. Randolph McDonald. p. 35

6 November 1798. Peter McDOWELL and Joannah Haley, dau. of Ambrose Haley who consents. Sur. Ambrose Haley, Jr. p. 25

11 December 1804. Andrew McHANEY and Polley Collins, dau. of Thomas Collins who consents. Sur. John Craddock. Married by Rev. Griffith Dickinson. p. 37

15 March 1805. John McHANEY and Elizabeth Mitchell. Married by Rev. Nathaniel Lovelace. p. 39

26 September 1786. William McKENNIE and Lucy Chick, dau. of William Chick who consents. Sur. Reubin Hubbard. Married by Rev. James Kinney. p. 8

24 August 1794. William McKINNEY and Rhodey Brown. Sur. Nathaniel Hubbard. p. 19

-- December 1801. Charles McLAUGHLIN and Alice Madding, dau. of Thomas Madding who consents. Sur. Eliaha Madding. Married by Rev. George Dodson. p. 31

3 March 1802. Joseph McMILLION and Polly Gravelly. Sur. William McMillion. Signs her own consent. Married by Rev. Clement Nance. p. 33

17 September 1794. Bird NANCE and Polley Hannah. Sur. Edward Phillips. Signs her own consent. Married by Rev. Lazarus Dodson. p. 19

12 January 1795. Isaac NANCE and Jane Smith. Sur. James Anderson. Signs her own consent. p. 21

12 August 1797. Mosias NANCE and Peggy Denton, dau. of James Denton who consents. Sur. William Shaw. p. 24

9 November 1782. William NANCE and Elizabeth Thornton. Married by Rev. Samuel Harris. p. 4

22 April 1801. William H. NANCE and Elizabeth V. Morton. Sur. Joseph Morton. Married by Rev. Clement Nance. p. 31

12 November 1790. John NASH and Betsey Hopper. Sur. Joseph Akin. Married by Rev. Richard Elliott. p. 13

23 March 1795. Robin NASH and Susanna Malicott. Sur. John Malicott. Mary Nash consents for Susanna. Married by Rev. Matthew Bates. p. 21

21 February 1801. Thomas NASH and Dice Malicoat, dau. of John Malicoat who consents. Sur. Edmund Mallicoat. p. 31

11 October 1783. William NASH and Catherine Tunbridge. Sur. William Owen. p. 5

21 September 1784. John NEAL and Elizabeth Stokes, dau. of Sillas Stokes who consents. Thomas Neal, father of John, also consents. Sur. Allen Stokes. p. 5

8 March 1801. John NEAL and Priscilla Craddock, dau. of John Craddock who consents. Sur. Robert Bumpass. p. 31

19 November 1804. Stephen NEAL and Sarah Craddock. Sur. N. Craddock. Married by Rev. Thomas Payne. p. 37

24 May 1782. John NEEL and Agness Midkiff. Married by Rev.
John Bailey. p. 4

19 February 1783. James NELSON and Mirrah Branner. Married
by Rev. Lazarus Dodson. p. 5

12 September 1803. Joel NELSON and Tabby Shockley. Sur. James
Shockley. Married by Rev. David Nowlin. p. 35

28 December 1803. John NELSON and Susey Boaz, dau. of Agness
Boaz who consents. Sur. Thomas Boaz. Married by Rev. David
Nowlin. p. 35

20 December 1802. Tapley NELSON and Charity Cox. Sur. John
Nelson. Signs her own consent. Married by Rev. Clement
Nance. p. 33

20 December 1781. William NELSON and ---- Rogers. Married by
Rev. John Bailey. p. 3

16 January 1792. William NELSON and Elizabeth Taylor. Sur.
Frederick Shelton. Signs her own consent. Married by Rev.
Matthew Bates. p. 16

11 October 1800. William NELSON and Susanna Corbin. Sur.
Bazel Nelson. Married by Rev. Richard Elliott. p. 29

24 February 1798. William NEWBILL, Jr., and Sarah Richardson.
Sur. Charles F. Walls. William Richardson guardian of Sarah
consents. p. 25

14 December 1801. Abel NEWBY and Elizabeth Hands. Sur.
Soloman Newby. Married by Rev. Elias Dodson. p. 31

29 September 1799. John NEWBY and Mary Hands. Sur. Rawley
Dodson. Signs her own consent. Married by Rev. George
Dodson. p. 27

9 November 1802. William NEWTON and Susanna Grubbs. Sur.
Jesse Rigney. Henry Newton signs certificate. Married by
Rev. Thomas Payne. p. 33

-- April 1781. John NORTON and Agness Gammon. Married by
Rev. Samuel Harris. p. 3

11 November 1796. John NORTON and Peechie Pulliam, dau. of
Drury Pulliam. Sur. Benjamin Pulliam. p. 22

12 February 1787. Bryant W. NOWLIN, Jr., and Bettey Towsend.
Sur. Thomas Towsend. Married by Rev. David Barr. p. 9

21 October 1790. Bryant W. NOWLIN and Mildred Hutchings.
Sur. James Hutchings. Christofor Hutchings consents for
Mildred. Married by Rev. Richard Elliott. p. 13

61

6 December 1794. David NOWLIN and Lucy Hensley. Sur. John Cook. p. 19

9 March 1804. David NOWLIN and Mary B. Bates. Sur. Thomas B. Jones. Married by Rev. Griffith Dickinson. p. 37

13 December 1792. James NOWLIN and Nancy Marlow, consent of James Downing (for which one?). Sur. Kinsey Marlow. Married by Rev. Matthew Bates. p. 16

21 February 1801. Richard NOWLIN and Selah Shelton, dau. of Armistead Shelton who consents. Sur. Stephen Shelton. p. 31

6 September 1786. Charles NICHOLAS and Marshall Farthing. Married by Rev. Lazarus Dodson. p. 8

20 June 1782. Julius NICKERN and Susannah Prewet. Married by Rev. Samuel Harris. p. 4

20 March 1792. John NUCKLES and Martha Prosize. Sur. George Watson. Married by Rev. Richard Elliott. p. 16

12 December 1792. Josiah NUCKLES and Milley Weatherford. Married by Rev. Richard Elliott. p. 16

16 July 1787. Barlett NUNNELLEE and Salley Johnson. Sur. R.C. Johnson. p. 9

10 ---- 1796. Isaac OAKES and Frances Thornton. Sur. Rowland Thornton. Married by Rev. Clement Nance. p. 22

-- ---- 1788. Thomas OAKES and ---- ----. Sur. Jesse Smith. p. 10

10 December 1797. William OAKES and Alcey Adkins. Sur. Edward Adkins. p. 24

30 August 1801. William OAKES and Ruth Smith. Sur. William Reynolds. p. 32

3 April 1802. Drury OLIVER and Elizabeth Daine, dau. of Jacob Daine who consents. Sur. William Daine. Married by Rev. Clement Nance. p. 33

15 May 1799. Matthew ORANDER and Sarah Brown, dau. of Frederick Brown who consents. Sur. Langston Brown. Married by Rev. Richard Elliott. p. 27

-- ---- 1790. Enoch ORGAN and Sarah Templeton. Married by Rev. John Jenkins. p. 13

18 April 1791. Matthew ORRENDUFF and Polley Bradley. Sur. Mastin Hardin. Married by Rev. Richard Elliott. p. 14

7 August 1786. Jesse OVERTON and Rachel Hamlett. Sur. Joseph Akin. Both sign their own certificates of consent. p. 8

18 August 1792. David OWEN and Peggey Nelson. Sur. John Nelson. p. 16

21 January 1793. Drury OWEN and Hedrick Mahue. Sur. West D. Hurt. Married by Rev. Matthew Bates. p. 17

20 July 1792. Obediah OWEN and Polly Legrand, dau. of Abraham Legrand who consents. Sur. John Owen. p. 16

26 December 1804. Pleasant OWEN and Sarah Jolly. Sur. William Jones. Signs her own consent. Married by Rev. John Jenkins. p. 37

24 February 1769. William OWEN and Edey Pigg, dau. of John Pigg. Sur. John Owen. p. 1

15 January 1802. Usse PANKEY and Sarah Kerby. Sur. John Kerby. p. 33

15 April 1805. David PARKER and Frankey Parker. Sur. Joseph Arthur. p. 39

29 December 1787. Samuel PARKS and Elizabeth Hutchings. John Parks guardian, consents. Sur. James Hutchings. Married by Rev. Samuel Harris. p. 9

22 March 1780. Thomas PARKS and Mary Parks. Sur. Joseph Akin. p. 3

24 December 1780. William PARKS and Caty Pain, dau. of Reuben Pain who consents. Sur. Joseph Wade. p. 3

5 November 1798. James PARRISH and Dorceas Hodges, dau. of Jesse Hodges who consents. Sur. Nicholas Parrish. Married by Rev. James Tompkins. p. 25

29 December 1803. John PARRISH and Keziah Stockton, dau. of John Stockton who consents. Sur. Peter Parish. p. 35

13 March 1785. Mose PARRISH and Mary Shaul. Married by Rev. Lazarus Dodson. p. 7

26 February 1805. Richard PARRISH and Jane Mitchell, dau. of Sarah Mitchell who consents. Sur. Edward Carter. Married by Rev. Richard Elliott. p. 39

6 October 1799. William PARRISH and Molley B. Thompkins, dau. of Mourning Tompkins who consents. Sur. John Thompkins. p. 27

12 July 1801. Jesse PARSON and Anna Mullins. Sur. Joshua Mullins. Married by Rev. Thomas Payne. p. 32

63

20 December 1790.   Benjamin PARSONS and Sarah Burton.   Sur.
Peter Thacker.   Elisha Burton consents for Sarah.   Married by
Rev. Richard Elliott.   p. 13

-- November 1791.   David PARSONS and Elizabeth Bailey.   Sur.
Joseph Parsons.   Signs her own consent.   Married by Rev. Richard
Elliott.   p. 14

2 November 1796.   Gabriel PARSONS and Sarah Justice, dau. of
William Justice who consents.   Sur. John Justice.   Married by
Rev. Thomas Douglas.   p. 22

26 February 1803.   John PARSONS, Jr., and Mishel Parsons,
dau. of Samuel Parsons, Sr., and Rebecker Parsons who consent.
Sur. Samuel Parsons.   Married by Rev. Griffith Dickinson.   p. 35

20 June 1791.   Joseph PARSONS and Sarah Adams.   Sur. Will
Adams.   Signs her own consent.   Married by Rev. Richard Elliott.
p. 14

15 October 1804.   Richard PARSONS and Milley Turley.   Married
by Rev. Thomas Payne.   Sur. John Turley.   p. 37

21 December 1779.   Samuel PARSONS and Beckey Farthing.   Sur.
William Parsons.   p. 2

14 December 1803.   Samuel PARSONS and Lucy Bailey, dau. of
Peter I. Bailey who consents.   Sur. David Parsons.   Married by
Rev. Richard Elliott.   p. 35

25 November 1805.   Thomas PARSONS and Sarah Parsons, dau. of
William and Mary Parsons who consent.   Sur. Samuel Parsons. p. 39

29 September 1800.   William PARSONS and Phebe Adkins, dau. of
Nathaniel Adkins who consents.   Sur. Jesse Adkins.   p. 29

24 April 1804.   James PATTERSON and Serene Trahern, dau. of
Nehemiah and Amelia Trahern who consent.   Sur. Samuel Trahern.
Married by Rev. Thomas Sparks who says Sweany.   p. 37

30 June 1794.   John PATTERSON and Polley Mustain.   Sur. Thomas
Dalton.   Married by Rev. Matthew Bates.   p. 19

-- ---- 1799.   William PATTERSON and Nancy Faris.   Married by
Rev. John Jenkins.   p. 27

16 June 1800.   Charles PAYNE and Leannah Fearn, dau. of Thomas
Fearn who consents.   Sur. Robert Payne.   p. 29

20 October 1784.   James PAYNE and Fanney Dix.   Sur. William
Wilkinson.   Married by Rev. Samuel Harris.   p. 5

6 December 1793. John PAYNE and Lucy Fearn, dau. of Thomas
Fearn who consents. Sur. Edmond Mitchell. p. 17

20 February 1795. John PAYNE and Milley Richards, dau. of
Gabriel Richards who consents. Sur. Archie Walters. p. 21

10 March 1800. John PAYNE and Sally Elliott, dau. of William
and Elizabeth Elliott who consent. Sur. Samuel Elliott. p. 29

24 May 1787. Phillimon PAYNE and Rachel Wilson. Sur. Reubin
Pain. Married by Rev. John Atkinson. p. 9

17 June 1793. Robert PAYNE and Elizabeth Lee Fearn, dau. of
Thomas Fearn who consents. Sur. William Tunstall. p. 18

16 October 1795. Thomas PAYNE and Sally Shelton. Sur. Armistead
Shelton. Signs her own consent. Married by Rev. Hawkins
Landrum. p. 21

17 June 1783. William PAYNE and Martha Dix, dau. of John Dix
who consents. Sur. Joseph Akin. p. 5

1 March 1802. William PAYNE and Maryan P. Griggory. Sur.
Giles Payne. p. 33

17 February 1785. Jesse PEAK and Peggy Shockley. Married by
Rev. David Barr. p. 7

29 January 1799. Jesse PEAK and Rhoda Adkins, dau. of William
Adkins who consents. Sur. Henry Adkins. p. 27

9 February 1796. John PEAK and Ruth Bell, dau. of John Bell
who consents. Sur. Thomas Bell. Married by Rev. Richard
Elliott. p. 22

2 February 1782. John PEARCE and Mary White. Married by Rev.
Samuel Harris. p. 4

18 August 1785. William PEARMAN and Mary Weldon. Sur.
Fortunatus Dodson. Signs her own consent. p. 6

20 February 1804. Sherwood PEARSON and Clarisa Wells. Sur.
Henry Wilson. p. 37

9 August 1785. John PEDOR and Elizabeth Crus. Married by
Rev. David Barr. p. 7

22 September 1790. John PEMBERTON and Ginsey Johnson. Sur.
James Mitchell. Isham Johnson consents for Ginsey. Married
by Rev. James Hurt. p. 13

-- ---- 1796. Henry PERKINS and Bethinia Cabell. Sur. David
Rice. p. 22

29 July 1802. Henry PERKINS and Bethania Cahall. Married by Rev. Clement Nance. p. 33

25 June 1798. John Pryor PERKINS and Elizabeth Harris, dau. of Samuel Harris who consents. Sur. Benjamin Harris. p. 25

25 October 1803. Thompson PHILLIPS and Sally Wood, dau. of Joseph Wood who consents and is surety. p. 35

24 October 1792. William PHILLIPS and Alee B. Henson. Sur. James Henson. Married by Rev. Thomas Douglas who says Alsey. p. 16

-- ---- 1800. William PHILLIPS and Elizabeth Henson. Married by Rev. Thomas Douglas. p. 29

22 October 1796. Edward PHILIPS and Jane Cunningham, dau. of Joseph Cunningham who consents. Sur. William Thomas. p. 22

6 September 1803. William PHLIPPIN and Tabitha Dodson, dau. of William Dodson who consents. Sur. Charles Shelton. Married by Rev. James Nelson. p. 35

17 October 1803. James PICKERALL and Lydia Butcher. Sur. William Butcher. Married by Rev. Griffith Dickinson. p. 35

24 December 1805. Thomas PICKERALL and Sally Dalton. Sur. Benjamin Dalton. Married by Rev. Willis Hopwood. p. 39

17 December 1804. Solomon PICKERELL and Anny Kezee, dau. of Jesse Keesee who consents. Sur. Lewis Dalton. Married by Rev. Willis Hopwood. p. 37

21 December 1801. Watte PICKERELL and Judith Dalton. Sur. Lewis Dalton. Married by Rev. Thomas Payne. p. 32

8 March 1793. Zadock PIERCE and Susanna Asten, dau. of Mary Asten who consents. Sur. Elijah Cummings. p. 17

12 October 1785. Hezekiah PIGG and Agness Owen, dau. of John Owen who consents. Elizabeth Pigg mother of Hezekiah consents. Sur. William Wright. p. 6

28 October 1787. John PIGG and Lucresia Payne. Married by Rev. Samuel Harris. p. 9

7 September 1789. Paul PIGG and Molley Holder. Sur. Joseph Wright. Signs her own consent. p. 11

5 June 1786. James PINKARD and Judith Smith. Sur. Peyton Smith. Married by Rev. David Barr. p. 8

20 July 1801. Thomas PINKARD and Salley Swanson, dau. of Will Swanson, Sr., who consents. Sur. Will Swanson, Jr. Married by Rev. John Wyatt. p. 32

3 October 1782. Abraham PISTOLE and Elizabeth Glasco. Married by Rev. Samuel Harris. p. 4

2 December 1800. James PISTOLE and Nelly Glascoe. Sur. Stephen Barber. John Long signs the certificate. Married by Rev. Richard Elliott. p. 29

20 September 1790. Thomas PISTOLE, Jr., and Lucy Reynolds. Sur. Richard Reynolds. Married by Rev. Richard Elliott. p. 13

10 July 1781. John PLATT and Vicry Tunbridge. Sur. John Pigg. Married by Rev. John Bailey. p. 3

21 September 1789. Thomas POINTER and Elizabeth Pruett. Sur. Thomas Shelton. Signs her own consent. p. 11

1 August 1804. John POLLARD and Polley Burnett. Sur. Barnett Burnett. Signs her own consent. Married by Rev. Richard Elliott. p. 37

21 March 1785. David POLLEY and Elizabeth Justice. Married by Rev. David Barr. p. 7

13 June 1785. Joseph POLLEY and Viney Midcalf. Married by Rev. David Barr. p. 7

13 November 1803. Nathaniel POPEJOY and Priscilla Matthews. Sur. Lake Matthews. Married by Rev. Richard Elliott. p. 35

16 April 1804. Robert POSEY and Jensey Farmer. Sur. Robert Hubbard. Married by Rev. John Jenkins. p. 37

15 June 1785. Benjamin POTTER and Elizabeth Bolton. Married by Rev. David Barr. p. 7

19 October 1796. Isaac POTTER and Salley Oakes. Sur. William Oakes. p. 22

3 July 1805. Robert POTTER and Lucey Harris, dau. of Charles Harris who consents. Sur. Reason B. White. Married by Rev. James Nelson. p. 39

29 May 1792. Ephraim POTTS and Elizabeth Bolling. Sur. Garland Hurt. Married by Rev. Matthew Bates. p. 16

19 July 1792. Elisha POWEL and Salley Thomas, dau. of Jonathan Thomas who consents. Sur. Henson Thomas. p. 16

30 March 1804. James POWELL and Anna Henry. Sur. Benjamin Henry. p. 37

7 January 1787. George PRATLEY and Lyda Dodson. Sur. James Johnson. Married by Rev. Lazarus Dodson. p. 9

21 September 1787. Joshua PRESTAGE and Elizabeth Gover. Sur. John Gover. p. 8

9 September 1793. John PREWET and Sarah Thomas. Sur. Henry Rowlins. p. 17

3 October 1778. Levy PREWET and Elizabeth Tailiaferro, dau. of John Tailiaferro who consents. Sur. James Akin. p. 2

11 February 1793. Abraham PREWETT and Rebecca Branson. Sur. William Branson. Consent of Heziah Branson for Rebecca. p. 17

25 September 1803. Absolom PREWETT and Betsey Elliott, dau. of John Elliott who consents. Sur. Arthur Johnson. Married by Rev. Richard Elliott. p. 35

22 February 1790, Arch PREWETT and Rebecca Blankinship. Sur. Charles Kendrick. Signs her own consent. p. 13

15 December 1795. Elijah PREWETT and Nancy Johnson. Married by Rev. Richard Elliott. p. 21

24 March 1790. Joseph PREWETT and Mary Elliott, dau. of Johnnithen Elliott who consents. Sur. Joseph Akin. Shouldn't this be Jonathan? p. 13

26 December 1788. Sam PREWITT, Jr., and Levina Walters. Sur. Robert Walters. Married by Rev. Richard Elliott. p. 10

15 June 1788. Culberth PRICE and Nancy Thompson, dau. of Ann Thompson who consents. Sur. Jennings Thompson. p. 10

26 November 1790. Daniel PRICE and Lucy Coleman, dau. of Stepehen Coleman who consents. Sur. Joseph Akin. p. 13

15 September 1794. Isaac PRICE and Crusey Dunn. Sur. John Dunn. p. 19

12 May 1801. Major PRICE and Salley Waller, dau. of John Waller who consents. Sur. Joel Waller. p. 32

27 December 1795. Maraday PRICE and Polley McDaniel. Sur. Peter Williams. p. 21

5 September 1788. Robert PRICE and Salley Church. Jonathan Church consents for Salley. Sur. Culberth Price. p. 10

24 January 1787. William Barber PRICE and Mary Polley Clark, dau. of Pattey Clark who consents. Sur. John Waller. p. 9

16 October 1797. Lim PRINDLE and Sally Brown, dau. of Henry and Sally Brown who consent. Sur. William Cookey. p. 24

12 March 1793. Richard PROCTOR and Winifred Short. Married by Rev. Richard Elliott. p. 18

26 November 1792. Thomas PROSIZE and Bettsey Adams. Sur. Nathan Adams. Married by Rev. Richard Elliott. p. 16

17 October 1785. Zechariah PRUIT and Jane Burgess, dau. of Edward Burgess who consents. Sur. Benjamin Thrasher. Married by Rev. Samuel Harris. p. 6

25 May 1792. John PRYON and Elizabeth Perkins, dau. of Peter Perkins who consents. Sur. William Astin. p. 16

11 November 1796. Benjamin PULLIAM and Elizabeth Norton, dau. of John Norton who consents and is surety. p. 22

27 November 1800. Robert PULLIAM and Betsy Clopton. Sur. Robert Pulliam. Married by Rev. John Atkinson. p. 29

26 July 1782. Joseph PYET and Sarah Still. Married by Rev. Thomas Sparks. p. 4

22 July 1782. Jeremiah PYRSON and Sarah Lambeth. Married by Rev. John Bailey. p. 4

23 December 1792. John QUINN and Ann Ashworth. Sur. Joshua Prewet. p. 16

9 March 1803. Richard QUINLEY and Nancy Odaniel. Sur. Levi Burton. Signs her own consent. Married by Rev. Clement Nance. p. 35

-- ---- 1805. Thomas RAGSDALE and Lucy Lanier, dau. of David Lanier. Married by Rev. Richard Elliott. P. 39. This bond is in Henry Co. Dated 18 Dec. 1805.

25 June 1802. Lewis RALPH and Peachy Headrick. Sur. Thomas Scarce. p. 33

17 January 1799. William Ramey and Lucy Alchols, widow. Sur. John Chattin. p. 27

17 March 1794. William RAMSEY and Rhoda McMillion. Sur. Nathan Sparks. Married by Rev. Thomas Sparks. p. 19

10 April 1797. Woodson RAMSEY and Salley Witcher, dau. of Daniel and Susanna Witcher who consent. Sur. Merlin Young. Married by Rev. Thomas Douglas. p. 24

21 November 1795. Henry RAWLINGS and Margaret Thomas (widow.) Sur. Joseph Thomas. Married by Rev. Richard Elliott. p. 21

24 October 1797. Isaac RAWLINS and Elizabeth Callam. Sur. Benjamin Bennett. p. 24

1 April 1782. Abraham RAZOR and Elizabeth Witcher. Married by Rev. John Bailey. p. 4

19 May 1779. David REECE and Nancy Cooley. Sur. Jacob Cooley. p. 2

30 September 1799. Daniel REAVES and Nancey Dodson. Sur. George Dodson. p. 27

21 September 1801. Hugh REYNOLDS and Elizabeth Mitchell, dau. of Sarah Mitchell who consents. Sur. Robert Devin. p. 32

21 August 1780. Joseph REYNOLDS and Margaret Devin. Sur. Edward Hodges. p. 3

26 July 1803. Joseph REYNOLDS and Nancy Ford. Sur. James Devin. Married by Rev. Richard Elliott. p. 35

2 March 1785. Richard REYNOLDS and Nancy Grisham. Married by Rev. David Barr. p. 7

16 March 1801. David RICE and Charity Briscoe. Sur. Will Tunstall. Signs her own consent. Married by Rev. Thomas Payne. p. 32

22 December 1797. Leonard RICE and Lydea Hawker, dau. of Ambrose and Liddy Hawker who consent. Sur. William Burgess. Consent says "Liddie". p. 24

15 September 1790. William RICE and Catharine Martin. Sur. John Martin. Married by Rev. Lazarus Dodson. p. 13

25 October 1793. William RICE and Dorcas Hanoon. Sur. Zachariah Butts. p. 18

16 March 1795. William RICE and Elizabeth Rogers. Sur. William Rogers. Signs her own consent. Married by Rev. Richard Elliott. p. 21

5 November 1804. William RICE and Susanna Brown, dau. of Henry Brown who consents. Sur. Hardin Chick. Married by Rev. John Jenkins. p. 38

7 November 1796. Jesse RICHARDS and Sally Campbell. Sur. Abraham Campbell. Married by Rev. Richard Elliott. p. 23

3 December 1805. George RICHARDSON and Miriam Dodson, dau. of
George Dodson who consents. Miriam also signs the certificate.
Sur. Thomas Walters. Married by Rev. Elias Dodson. p. 39

2 September 1799. Henry RICHARDSON and Judith Hollagan, dau.
of William and Judah Holligan who consent. Sur. Richard Mitchell.
Married by Rev. Clement Nance. p. 27

15 April 1799. John RICHARDSON and Nancy Pulliam, dau. of
Drewry Pulliam who consents. Sur. James C. Burnett. p. 27

18 April 1798. Joshua RICHARDSON and Polley Burnett, dau. of
James Burnett. Sur. John Burnett. Married by Rev. Clement
Nance. p. 25

21 March 1803. William RICHARDSON and Elizabeth Shields, dau.
of Pleasand and Elizabeth Shields who consent. Sur. William
Walters. p. 35

4 June 1789. William RICKETS and Nancy Davis. Sur. John
Davis. William Davis consents for Nancy. Married by Rev.
Richard Elliott. p. 11

15 February 1800. John RICKETT and Betsey Ivey. Sur. John
Chattin. Married by Rev. Richard Elliott. p. 30

23 October 1798. James RICKETTS and Elizabeth Oaks. Sur.
James Soyars. Married by Rev. James Tompkins. p. 25

-- ---- 1804. James RIDGEWAY and Ann Henderson. Married by
Rev. John Jenkins. p. 38

-- ---- 1790. John RIDGEWAY and Anne Compton. Married by
Rev. John Jenkins. p. 13

12 September 1788. Jonathan RIDGEWAY and Elizabeth Shields.
John Shields consents for Elizabeth. Sur. John Shackleford.
p. 10

29 January 1805. Griffith RIGNEY and Lavina Taylor, dau. of
James Taylor who consents. Sur. William Taylor. Married by
Rev. Willis Hopwood. p. 39

4 November 1795. Jesse RIGNEY and Elizabeth Linthicum. Sur.
Thomas Linthicum. Married by Rev. Richard Elliott. p. 21

27 January 1788. John RIGNEY and Catharine Huffman. Married
by Rev. James Hinton. p. 10

20 January 1789. John RIGNEY and ---- ----. Sur. William
Griffith. p. 11

10 December 1788. Absolom RILEY and Jane Faris, dau. of
John Faris who consents. Sur. John Gwin. p. 10

6 September 1804. Hezekiah RIPLEY and Polley Dove. Sur. Leonard Dove. Levi and Sarah Bow sign certificate. Married by Rev. Griffith Dickinson. p. 38

-- ---- 1795. Burdet ROACH and Elizabeth Mitchell. Married by Rev. Matthew Bates. p. 21

30 July 1792. James ROACH and Mary Barrot. Sur. John Barrot. Married by Rev. Matthew Bates. p. 16

14 December 1782. James ROBERSON and Charlot Holton. Married by Rev. John Bailey. p. 4

20 March 1786. Daniel ROBERTS and Mary George. Sur. Joseph Akin. p. 8

11 December 1781. Ezra ROBERTS and Patty Brewer, dau. of James Brewer who consents. Sur. Joseph Akin. Married by Rev. John Bailey. p. 3

1 October 1785. Samuel ROBERTS and Sally Jordan Cooley. Married by Rev. David Barr. p. 7

16 September 1805. Fielding ROBERTSON and Milley Dodson. Sur. John Thompson. Married by Rev. William Blair. p. 39

30 October 1781. James ROBERTSON and Sarah Coleman. Married by Rev. John Bailey. p. 3

28 March 1771. Jesse ROBERTSON and Betsey Pigg, dau. of John Pigg who consents. Sur. John Cox. p. 1

19 March 1798. Meredith ROBERTSON and Jane Cunningham, dau. of Thomas Cunningham who consents. Sur. Ephraim Cunningham. Married by Rev. Clement Nance. p. 25

7 August 1801. Samuel ROBERTSON and Sally Hudson, dau. of John and Sarah Hudson who consent. Sur. Henry Polley. p. 32

18 January 1802. Allen ROBINSON and Milley Parsons. Sur. William Parsons. p. 33

30 January 1798. John ROBINSON and Nelley Muckmillion, dau. of Aspen Muckmillion who consents. Sur. Thomas Curry. Surely this is McMillion. p. 25

26 July 1800. John ROBINSON and Jenny Hollagan, dau. of William and Judith Holligan who consent. Sur. William Hollagan, Jr. Married by Rev. Clement Nance. p. 30

2 October 1781. William ROBINSON and Esther Stowe. Sur.
Joseph Akin. Signs her own consent. p. 3

5 December 1782. William ROBINSON and Prudence Russell.
Married by Rev. Lazarus Dodson. p. 4

-- ---- 1791. Josiah ROGERS and Elizabeth Smith. Married by
Rev. Richard Elliott. p. 14

27 January 1795. Josiah ROGERS and Elizabeth Richards, dau.
of Joseph Richards who consents. Sur. William Rogers. p. 21

23 August 1798. Reubin ROGERS and Hannah Price. Sur. John
Price. p. 25

-- ---- 1803. Stephen ROGERS and Nancy Billings. Married by
Rev. Richard Elliott. p. 35

22 January 1789. William ROGERS and Nancy Brawner. Married
by Rev. Lazarus Dodson. p. 11

5 January 1804. Robert ROLAND and Sarah Dudley. Married by
Rev. Griffith Dickinson. p. 38

-- ---- 1799. Henry ROLLEN and Nancy Rollen. Married by
Rev. John Jenkins. p. 27

11 August 1789. Abraham RORER and Nancy Cook. Sur. Thomas
Dyer. p. 11

21 January 1793. David RORER and Betsey Debo, dau. of Philip
Debo who consents. Sur. John White. p. 18

21 March 1795. Jonathan ROSSELL and Anna P. Watson, dau. of
John Watson who consents. Sur. Joab Watson. Married by Rev.
Richard Elliott. p. 21

6 January 1790. Joseph ROWDEN and Susanna Adams. Married by
Rev. Richard Elliott. p. 13

27 December 1785. Laban ROWDEN and Milley Adams, dau. of
Mourning Adams who consents (mother). Sur. William Short.
Married by Rev. Samuel Harris. p. 7

-- ---- 1800. Nathan ROWLAND and Eunice Faris. Married by
Rev. John Jenkins. p. 30

7 November 1796. Kennon RUMBLE and Elizabeth Watson. Sur.
John Watson. Married by Rev. Richard Elliott. p. 23

6 September 1791. Ezekiel RUSSELL and Martha Wright. Married
by Rev. Lazarus Dodson. p. 14

19 December 1796. George RUSSELL and Margaret Walters. Sur. Ezekial Russell. p. 23

10 July 1789. Matthew RUSSELL and Susanna Dupea. Married by Rev. Lazarus Dodson. p. 11

6 January 1792. Philip RUSSELL and Elizabeth Stewart. Sur. Thomas Williams. Martha Stewart consents for Elizabeth p. 16

-- ---- 1794. Richard RUSSELL and Isabel Stuart. Married by Rev. Matthew Bates. p. 19

19 January 1789. Samuel RUSSELL and Susannah Hundley. Sur. William Childris. p. 11

21 April 1792. William RUSSELL and Sarah Dupey. Married by Rev. Lazarus Dodson. p. 16

25 December 1801. William RUSSELL and Sarah Dodson. Married by Rev. Elias Dodson. p. 32

30 August 1773. William RYBURN and Mary Terry. Sur. Ben Terry. Signs her own consent. p. 1

20 March 1770. Lewis SALMON and Margaret Shannon, dau. of Thomas Shannon who consents. Sur. John Salmon. p. 1

19 September 1785. Edward SAMUEL and Elizabeth Harrison. Sur. William Dix. Married by Rev. Samuel Harris. p. 7

-- ---- 1787. William SANDERS and Ann Dove. Sur. Thomas Lester. Signs her own consent. p. 9

3 January 1783. William SARGE and Nancy Furbush. Married by Rev. John Bailey. p. 5

-- August 1783. John SARTAIN and Anner Adkson. Married by Rev. John Bailey. Shouldn't this be Adkerson? p. 5

8 November 1804. Daniel SAUNDERS and Frances Davis, dau. of Thomas Davis who consents. Sur. George Davis. Married by Rev. Griffith Dickinson. p. 38

30 December 1804. Henry SAUNDERS and Nancy Love, dau. of James Love who consents and is surety. Married by Rev. Griffith Dickinson. p. 38

3 March 1798. Jacob SAUNDERS and Seludy Davis, dau. of Thomas Davis who consents. Sur. George Davis. Married by Rev. Thomas Payne. p. 25

18 August 1788. Jesse SAUNDERS and Phebe Rowland. p. 11

16 December 1793. James SAWYERS and Jane Oakes. Sur. Siller Stokes. p. 18

29 December 1786. William SAWYERS and Lucrecia Cross. Married by Rev. Samuel Harris. p. 8

19 January 1802. Thomas SCARCE and Christina Harp. Sur. Zadock Pearce. p. 33

25 November 1800. Clement SCOTT and Salley Slaydon, dau. of William and Nancy Slaydon who consent. Sur. Arthur Slaydon. Married by Rev. George Dodson. p. 30

10 December 1789. James SCOTT and Rebecca Streetman, dau. of Elizabeth Streetman who consents. Sur. James Gammon. p. 12

28 February 1782. John SCOTT and Saphira Murry. Married by Rev. Samuel Harris. p. 4

2 April 1782. John SCOTT and Eleanor Vandevor. Married by Rev. James Robinson. p. 4

17 October 1799. Samuel Milton SCOTT and Sally Bruce. Married by Rev. Thomas Payne. p. 27

14 July 1805. Gross SCRUGGS and Elizabeth Gilbert. Married by Rev. Griffith Dickinson. p. 39

25 August 1805. Thomas SCRUGGS and Eda Dejarnet. Married by Rev. Nathaniel Lovelace. p. 39

7 January 1782. Solomon SEAL and Susannah Hall. Married by Rev. John Bailey. p. 4

24 August 1789. John SEALS and Margaret Hall, dau. of Jean Hall who consents. Consent of William Seals for John. Sur. Zachariah Seals. p. 11

23 October 1790. William SEALS, Jr., and Eliza. Hawker. Sur. John Givings. This should be Elizabeth. p. 13

7 January 1805. Parham SEMORE and Frances H. Shelton, dau. of Thomas Shelton who consents. Sur. Elijah Creel. Married by Rev. George Dodson. p. 40

8 October 1782. Thomas SERGE and Milley Adkins. Married by Rev. John Bailey. p. 4

13 June 1784. William SERVANT and Barbary Oneal. Married by Rev. John Bailey. p. 6

31 March 1799. Jacob SEWELL and Lucy Nelson. Sur. Thomas Cecill. Married by Rev. Elias Dodson. p. 27

SEYMOUR: See Semore

9 December 1795. Abner SHACKLEFORD and Frances Wright. Sur. John Bennett. p. 21

13 September 1784. Henry SHACKLEFORD and Mary Shields. Married by Rev. David Barr. p. 6

28 January 1785. John SHACKLEFORD and Jeane Shields, dau. of John Shields who consents. Sur. Joshua Cantrell. Married by Rev. David Barr. p. 7

26 December 1804. Alexander SHAW and Elizabeth Blair. Sur. William James. Signs her own consent. Married by Rev. Robert Hurt. p. 38

25 August 1801. Evan SHAW and Rhoda Nelson. Sur. Robert Wright. p. 32

8 May 1789. Francis SHAW and Nancy Steward. Married by Rev. Lazarus Dodson. p. 11

4 December 1801. Robert SHAW and Anne Nash, dau. of John Nash who consents. Sur. Sam Guyer. p. 32

23 February 1795. William SHAW and Susanna Nance, dau. of Clement Nance who consents. Sur. Mosias (Moses?) Nance. p. 21

17 December 1792. Abraham SHELTON and Lettice Shelton, dau. of John Shelton who consents. Sur. Fred Shelton. Married by Rev. Hawkins Landum. p. 16

1 September 1774. Armistead SHELTON and Susannah Shelton, dau. of Daniel Shelton who consents. Sur. Joseph Akin. p. 1

25 December 1769. Beverly SHELTON and Ann Coleman. Sur. Gabriel Shelton. Signs her own consent. p. 1

8 August 1803. Beverly SHELTON and Olive Shelton, dau. of Armistead Shelton who consents. Sur. Beverly Shelton. Gabriel Shelton, father of Beverly, consents. Married by Rev. Thomas Payne. p. 35

31 October 1803. Beverly SHELTON, Jr., and Ritta Shelton, dau. of Armistead Shelton who consents. Sur. Beverly Shelton. Married by Rev. Thomas Payne. p. 35

17 March 1800. Charles SHELTON and Elizabeth Flippin. Sur. Joseph Flippin. Married by Rev. Richard Elliott. p. 30

16 May 1785. Clabron SHELTON and Luedy Mustain, dau. of Thomas Mustain who consents. Sur. Robert Tucker. p. 7

27 July 1797. Coleman SHELTON and Elizabeth Shelton. Married
by Rev. Thomas Payne. p. 24

21 July 1785. Daniel SHELTON and Elizabeth Garner. Married
by Rev. David Barr. p. 7

18 June 1792. Daniel SHELTON and Martha Keatts, dau. of John
Keatts who consents. Sur. Leroy Shelton. Married by Rev.
Matthew Bates. p. 16

30 May 1785. David SHELTON and Elizabeth Shields, dau. of
John Shields who consents. Sur. Moses Vincent. p. 7

21 July 1800. David SHELTON and Rhoda Hurt. Sur. Benjamin
Shelton. Elizabeth Shelton mother of David. Married by Rev.
Thomas Payne. p. 30

16 October 1795. Frederick SHELTON and Polley Shelton. Sur.
Armistead Shelton. Signs her own consent. Married by Rev.
Thomas Payne. p. 21

29 June 1794. Gabriel SHELTON and Mary Beuford. Sur. Reddick
Shelton. Signs her own consent. Married by Rev. Thomas
Payne. p. 19

24 September 1799. Gabriel SHELTON, Jr., and Rachel Sheppard,
dau. of William Shepard who consents and is surety. p. 27

13 June 1803. George SHELTON and Elizabeth Farmer. Sur.
Elijah Creel. Signs her own consent. p. 36

17 December 1792. Griggory SHELTON and Elizabeth Bewford,
dau. of Mary Bewford who consents. Sur. Fred Shelton.
Shouldn't this be Gregory and Buford? p. 16

19 December 1803. Henry R. SHELTON and Elizabeth L. Morgan,
dau. of Mary Morgan who consents. Sur. Michel Roberts. Married
by Rev. Griffith Dickinson. p. 35

17 March 1794. John M. SHELTON and Rebecca Shelton. Sur.
Thomas Lankford. Married by Rev. Thomas Payne. p. 19

12 May 1800. John SHELTON and Sarah McLaughlin, dau. of
Charles and Sarah McLaughlin who consent. Sur. Joel Slayden.
Married by Rev. Elias Dodson. p. 30

28 May 1804. John SHELTON and Anne Payne. Sur. Abel Wilson.
Signs her own consent. Abel Wilson is designated as "guardian".
Of which one? Married by Rev. George Dodson. p. 38

3 September 1803. Josiah SHELTON and Nancy Ross, dau. of
William Ross who consents. Sur. Thomas Elliott. Married by
Rev. Thomas Sparks. p. 36

77

2 August 1796. Lemuel SHELTON and Lettice W. Shelton, dau. of Beverly Shelton who consents. Sur. Roddick Shelton. p. 23

19 December 1785. Leonard SHELTON and Susannah Roberts, dau. of Joseph Roberts who consents. Sur. Vincent Shelton. p. 7

1 March 1805. Levi SHELTON and Frances E. Echols, dau. of Moses Echols who consents. Frances also signs the certificate. Sur. Evans Echols. Married by Rev. Richard Elliott. p. 40

7 December 1803. Reddick SHELTON and Nancy Shelton. Sur. West D. Hurt. Signs her own consent. Married by Rev. Thomas Payne. p. 35

16 July 1792. Richard SHELTON and Nancy Shelton. Sur. William Clark. Married by Rev. Hawkins Landrum. p. 16

22 August 1798. Stephen SHELTON and Lettice Shelton. Gabriel Shelton, father (of which one?). Armistead Shelton signs certificate. Sur. Abraham Shelton. p. 25

21 April 1798. Taliaferro SHELTON and Jane Irby. Married by Rev. Thomas Payne. p. 26

20 November 1804. Tabernor SHELTON and Peggy Arch Deacon. Sur. George Adams. Married by Rev. William Davis. p. 38

10 January 1785. Thomas SHELTON and Nancey Hurt, dau. of Moses Hurt who consents. Sur. Leroy Shelton. p. 7

18 March 1805. Thomas SHELTON and Mary Burch, dau. of John Burch who consents. Sur. Thomas Shelton, Jr. Married by Rev. James Nelson. p. 40

15 December 1794. Tunstall SHELTON and Fanney Payne, dau. of Thomas Payne who consents. Sur. Young Shelton. Married by Rev. Thomas Payne. p. 19

1 May 1805. Washington SHELTON and Susanna Williams. Sur. John Williams. Married by Rev. Thomas Payne. p. 40

29 October 1786. William SHELTON and Martisha Taylor. Sur. Abraham Shelton. Signs her own consent. Married by Rev. Lazarus Dodson. p. 8

3 May 1791. William SHELTON and Elizabeth C. Johnson, dau. of James Johnson who consents. Sur. Frederick Shelton. Married by Rev. James Hurt. p. 14

-- December 1798. William SHELTON and Priscilla Mustain. Sur. William Price. p. 26

12 February 1795. Young SHELTON and Betsy Lewis. Married by Rev. Thomas Payne. p. 21

7 March 1796. William SHEPPARD and Polley F. Taylor. Sur.
Richard Johnson. p. 23

27 April 1805. John SHIELDS and Elizabeth Hayns. Sur. Thomas
Crews. Signs her own consent. Married by Rev. David Nowlin.
p. 40

23 December 1786. Littleberry Shields and Susannah Rogers.
Sur. Isham Farmer. p. 8

16 April 1787. Thomas SHIELDS and Mary Cunningham. Sur.
Joseph Cunningham. Married by Rev. David Barr. p. 10

12 September 1803. James SHOCKLEY and Peggy Thomas. Sur.
Jonathan Thomas. Married by Rev. Richard Elliott. p. 35

11 December 1798. Robert SHOCKLEY and Belinda Elliott. Sur.
William Elliott. Married by Rev. James Tompkins. p. 25

25 December 1797. Abner SHORT and Patty Giles. Sur. John
Giles, Jr. Abner son of William Short. p. 24

31 August 1802. Isaac SHORT and Milley Richards, dau. of Joseph
Richards who consents. Sur. Abner Short. p. 33

17 December 1793. Josiah SHORT and Jobil Crane, dau. of John
Crane who consents. Sur. William Short. p. 18

16 October 1789. William SHORT and Jane Kimens. Sur. Thomas
Ragsdale. p. 11

21 December 1798. Fielding SHUMATE and Susanna Elliott, dau.
of Jonathan Elliott who consents. Sur. Joshua Prewitt. p. 25

6 August 1801. Francis SIMPSON and Ritter Shelton. Married
by Rev. Thomas Payne. p. 32

20 December 1790. Loyd SIMPSON and Martha Smith, dau. of
Martha Smith who consents. Sur. Jesse Smith. Married by
Rev. Richard Elliott. p. 13

16 December 1805. Thomas SIMPSON and Frances Slayden, dau.
of Joseph Slayden who consents. Sur. William Simpson. Married
by Rev. Elias Dodson. p. 40

7 November 1803. William SIMPSON and Letty Walters, dau. of
Robert Walters who consents. Sur. Thomas Stamps. Married by
Rev. Elias Dodson. p. 35

4 June 1787. Price SKINNER and Salley Mustain, dau. of Thomas
and Mary Mustain who consent. Sur. Thomas Davis. p. 9

19 December 1796. William SLATE and Carolin M. Clark. Sur. Joseph Clark. p. 23

11 November 1802. Daniel E. SLAYDON and Elley Boyd, dau. of Thomas and Judy Boyd who consent. Sur. Thomas Slaydon. p. 33

3 October 1805. Daniel SLATON and Milly Dalton. Sur. Thomas Hardey. Married by Rev. George Dodson. p. 40

20 February 1797. Joel SLATON and Mary McLaughlin, dau. of Charles and Sarah McLaughlin who consent. Sur. David Dodson. Married by Rev. George Dodson. p. 24

29 September 1800. Thomas SLAYDEN and Rachel Slayden, dau. of Joseph and Milley Slayden who consent. Sur. Obediah Slayden. p. 30

19 December 1796. Arthur SLAYDON and Lucy Shelton, dau. of Thomas Shelton who consents. Arthur son of Daniel Slaydon. Sur. William Slaydon. Married by Rev. George Dodson. p. 23

16 December 1799. John SLAYDON and Betsy Walters, dau. of Robert Walters who consents. Sur. Charles Collie. p. 27

26 March 1793. Arthur SLAYTON and Nancy Spratling. Sur. Billey Holloway. p. 18

17 March 1794. Daniel SLAYTON and Elizabeth Hendrick. Sur. Jesse Mann. p. 19

23 April 1782. James SLAYTON and Martha Pigg. Married by Rev. John Bailey. p. 4

17 October 1784. James SLOAN and Polley Justice. Married by Rev. David Barr. p. 6

21 April 1804. Booker SMITH and Elizabeth Smith, dau. of Francis Smith who consents and is surety. p. 38

27 October 1782. George SMITH and Delilah Thomason. Sur. Joseph Akin. p. 5

7 April 1786. Hezekiah SMITH and Salley Leftwich, dau. of Thomas Leftwich who consents. Sur. Drewry Smith. p. 8

18 December 1788. James SMITH and Mary Hammock. Married by Rev. Lazarus Dodson. p. 11

18 January 1802. James SMITH and Judith Smith. Sur. James Bruce. Ralph Smith signs certificate. Married by Rev. Thomas Payne. p. 33

7 December 1790. John SMITH and Agness Stockton. Married by Rev. Richard Elliott. p. 13

28 November 1797. John SMITH and Polley Shields. Sur. William
Tunstall. Signs her own consent. p. 24

19 May 1795. Joseph SMITH and Barsha Humphrey, dau. of James
Humphrey who consents. Sur. Ezra Walters. p. 21

28 May 1797. Joseph SMITH and Susanna Thurman, dau. of John
and Nancy Thurman who consent. Sur. Edmund Boaz. p. 24

10 October 1805. Joseph SMITH and Elitha Fowlkes, dau. of
James and Salley Fowlkes who consent. Sur. Caleb Anglin. p. 40

13 October 1778. Lemuel SMITH and Bethania Perkins, dau. of
Peter Perkins who consents. Sur. Joseph Akin. p. 2

16 December 1769. Mumford SMITH and Catherine Armstrong. Sur.
John Gregory. p. 1

4 November 1789. Peter SMITH and Barbary Brevins. Married by
Rev. Lazarus Dodson. p. 11

21 May 1792. Samuel SMITH and Sarah Ward. Sur. Will Tunstall,
Jr. p. 16

6 August 1781. William SMITH and Patsey Russell. Married by
Rev. Lewis Shelton. p. 3

27 July 1787. William SMITH and Jane Stuard. Married by
Rev. Lazarus Dodson. p. 10

-- ---- 1790. William SMITH and Elizabeth Rodd. Married by
Rev. John Jenkins. p. 13

19 August 1797. William SMITH and Sally Sutherlin. Sur.
Adams Sutherlin. p. 24

13 October 1797. William SMITH and Patsey Asher, dau. of
Nathane Asher who consents. Sur. Miller Aster. p. 24

18 October 1802. William SMITH and Lucy Westbrook. Sur.
Stephen Yates. Signs her own consent. Married by Rev. Griffith
Dickinson. p. 33

19 August 1805. William SMITH and Elizabeth Brunett, dau. of
Henry Burnett who consents. Elizabeth Also signs certificate.
Sur. James Blakeley. p. 40

10 September 1785. George SNAUGH and Peggy Oneal, dau. of
Susannah Oneal who consents. Sur. George Dyer. p. 7

12 December 1804. William SNODDY and Virlena Burgess, dau.
of Edward Burgess who consents. Sur. William Burgess. Married
by Rev. David Nowlin. p. 38

-- ---- 1785. Mark SNOW snd Elizabeth Terrance. Married by
Rev. Nathaniel Thurman. p. 7

21 November 1790. William SOUTHERLAND and Nancy Gwin, dau. of
George H. Gwin who consents. Sur. John Gwin. Married by Rev.
Samuel Harris. p. 13

14 February 1805. William SOYARS and Joyce Price, dau. of
William Price, Sr., who consents. Sur. William Price. Married
by Rev. Richard Elliott. p. 40

27 November 1804. Edmund SPARKS and Patsey Wright. Sur.
Nathan Sparks. Married by Rev. Thomas Sparks. p. 38

14 August 1792. John SPARKS and Catherine Baggerley. Sur.
David Baggerley. p. 16

7 January 1794. Josiah SPARKS and Susannah Phillips, dau. of
Thomas Phillips who consents. Sur. Matthew Sparks. Married
by Rev. Thomas Sparks. p. 19

28 November 1802. Matthew B. SPARKS and Nancy Sutton. Sur.
William Booth. p. 33

4 October 1788. True Love SPARKS and Jane Sparks, dau. of
Martha Sparks who consents. Sur. Peter Pigg. p. 11

18 April 1785. John SPENCER and Molly Clopton, dau. of Robert
Clopton who consents and is surety. p. 7

15 January 1805. William SPENCER and Milly Alexander. William
Alexander consents for Milly. Sur. George Inge. Married by
Rev. Thomas Payne. p. 40

15 February 1802. Hickman SPILLER and Sally Payne, dau. of
William Payne who consents. Sur. James Colyuhoun. p. 34

19 December 1791. William SPRAGINS and Nancy Watkins, dau.
of Stephen Watkins who consents. Sur. Money Weatherford. p. 14

19 December 1803. Timothy STAMPS and Leah Wilson, dau. of
John Wilson who consents. Sur. Thomas Vaughn. p. 36

7 October 1784. Joseph STANDLEY and Elizabeth Mays. Married
by Rev. David Barr. p. 6

3 February 1784. Robert STANIFORD and Betsy Ann Watson.
Married by Rev. Thomas Sparks. p. 5

9 October 1792. Isaac STANLEY and Frances Nash. Sur. John
Nash. Married by Rev. Matthew Bates. p. 16

3 October 1789.   John STANSFIELD and Susanna Harrison, dau. of
Sarah Harrison who consents.   Sur. William Harrison.   p. 12

28 December 1797.   Thomas STEGALD and Marriam Harris, dau.
of George Harris who consents.   Sur. Peter Harris.   p. 24

4 November 1799.   Reubin STEPHENS and Edy Hubbard, dau. of
Hezakiah Hubbard who consents.   Sur. Adin Gray.   Married by
Rev. Thomas Douglas.   p. 27

26 March 1800.   Thomas STEWART and Patsy W. Worsham.   Sur.
Thomas Wilkinson.   p. 30

17 December 1799.   Joel STOE and Hannah Morrice.   Sur. William
Morrice.   p. 27

-- ---- 1797.   Joel STOKES and Salley Wright.   Sur. Richard
Elliott.   Sillas Stokes, Sr., signs the certificate.   Married
by Rev. Richard Elliott.   p. 24

16 December 1793.   Sylvanus STOKES and Nancy Price.   Sur. James
Sowyers.   p. 18

1 September 1803.   Benjamin STONE and Archer Parham.   Sur.
William G. Parham.   Signs her own consent.   p. 36

18 June 1795.   Hendley STONE and Jane Payne Harrison, dau.
of William Harrison who consents.   Sur. John Traharn.   Married
by Rev. Clement Nance.   p. 21

26 May 1798.   Hensley STONE and Elizabeth Pryor (widow), dau.
of Peter Perkins.   Sur. Aquilla Wilson.   p. 26

3 September 1803.   James H. STONE and Elizabeth Fitzgerald.
Sur. James Fitzgerald.   Edmond Fitzgerald consents for
Elizabeth.   p. 35

6 December 1802.   John STONE and Lucy Neal (widow).   Sur.
David Neal.   Signs her own consent.   p. 33

15 December 1795.   Joshua STONE, Jr., and Prudence Mottley.
Married by Rev. John Jenkins.   p. 21

30 January 1783.   Samuel STONE and Abbygie Fitzgerald.   Married
by Rev. John Bailey.   Shouldn't this be Abigail?   p. 5

22 April 1804.   Thomas C. STONE and Jenny Mason.   Sur. Isaac
Robertson.   Married by Rev. Griffith Dickinson.   p. 38

27 August 1804.   James STILL and Nancy Boaz.   Married by Rev.
William Davis.   p. 38

2 October 1785. Nathan SULLINS and Elizabeth Farmer. Married by Rev. Lazarus Dodson. p. 7

24 December 1799. Samuel SUMMERS and Polley Price. Sur. John Price. Married by Rev. Richard Elliott. p. 27

20 December 1801. Adam SUTHERLIN and Betsey Robertson. Sur. Edward Robertson. p. 32

16 June 1800. George SUTHERLIN, Jr., and Polley Mickelburrough, dau. of Henry Mickelburrough who consents. Sur. V. Wright. p. 30

23 February 1782. William SUTTEN and Martha Norton. Married by Rev. Thomas Sparks. p. 4

21 November 1803. Francis SWANSON and Fanny Chatten Muse. Sur. Thomas Muse. Married by Rev. Richard Elliott. p. 35

15 June 1801. William SWANSON, Jr., and Elizabeth Muse, dau. of John Muse who consents. Sur. Joseph Carter. p. 32

2 May 1782. Henry SWEDEVENT and Mary Bucknell. Married by Rev. John Bailey. p. 4

9 August 1784. Joseph SWEENEY and Nancy Maples. Married by Rev. Lazarus Dodson. p. 6

6 March 1790. John SWEPSTON and Dolly Ashfurd. Sur. John Buckley. Signs her own consent. Married by Rev. James Hurt. p. 13

15 August 1796. John SWINNEY and Lydia Polley. Sur. David Polley. Married by Rev. Thomas Payne. p. 23

1 April 1796. Joseph SWINNEY and Rebecca Allen. Sur. Joseph Akin. Godfrey Burnett signs certificate. Married by Rev. Thomas Payne. p. 23

23 January 1796. Moses SWINNEY and Pattsey Cooper. Sur. Joseph Akin. p. 23

1 March 1794. Aveal SYKES and Amy Hudson. Sur. William Hudson. p. 19

23 August 1803. John TALBERT and Nancy Irby. Sur. Joseph Mottley. Signs her own consent. p. 36

20 June 1795. Thomas TANNER and Nancey Powell, dau. of Mary Herring who consents. Sur. William Herring. p. 21

18 July 1785. Daniel TAYLOR and Drucilla Rigney. Married by Rev. David Barr. p. 7

1 April 1775. Edmund TAYLOR and Millicent Shelton, dau. of Daniel Shelton who consents and is surety. p. 1

25 July 1797. James TAYLOR and Jane Shelton, dau. of Gabriel Shelton who consents. Sur. Griggory Shelton. Married by Rev. Thomas Payne. p. 24

10 November 1804. James TAYLOR and Jincey Crutchfield. Sur. Jeremiah Keesee. p. 38

11 July 1782. John TAYLOR and Blanch Bucknell. Married by Rev. John Bailey. p. 4

10 December 1793. Joseph TAYLOR and Elizabeth Ford. Sur. Samuel Hughes. Signs her own consent. Married by Rev. Richard Elliott. p. 18

-- ---- 1804. William TAYLOR and Jincey Keesee. Married by Rev. Richard Elliott. p. 38

19 March 1792. Martin TEMPLETON and Nancy King. Sur. Hardin Chick. Signs her own consent. p. 16

1 December 1805. Johnson TERRELL and Elizabeth Terrell. Married by Rev. Henry Brown. p. 40

4 February 1805. Barton TERRY and Mary Walters, dau. of Archibald Walters who consents. Sur. Clement Scott. Married by Rev. Elias Dodson. p. 40

15 December 1794. Benjamin TERRY and Delilah Mottley. Sur. William Parker. Married by Rev. Lazarus Dodson. p. 19

7 January 1783. Charles TERRY and Judah Terry. Married by Rev. Lazarus Dodson. p. 5

5 January 1799. David TERRY and Lettice Nash, dau. of John and Anna Nash who consent. Sur. Tarpley Yeatts. p. 27

7 January 1805. Jeremiah TERRY and Fanny Clopton. Sur. A.W. Clopton. Married by Rev. Griffith Dickinson. p. 40

3 December 1782. John TERRY and Sarah Hodnett. Married by Rev. Lazarus Dodson. p. 4

20 April 1789. John TERRY and Mary Shaw. Sur. John King. Signs her own consent. Married by Rev. Lazarus Dodson. p. 12

19 July 1792. John TERRY and Milley Steward. Married by Rev. Lazarus Dodson. p. 16

-- ---- 1799. John TERRY and Sally Neal. Married by Rev. John Jenkins. p. 28

22 April 1784. Thomas TERRY and Mary Thomson. Married by Rev. Lazarus Dodson. p. 6

-- ---- 1785. Thomas TERRY and Nancy Dalton. Married by
Rev. Nathaniel Thurman. p. 7

6 December 1800. Absolom THACKER and Nancy Atkins. Sur.
Nathaniel Adkins. Married by Rev. Richard Elliott. p. 30

14 February 1804. Anderson THACKER and Selah Robertson. Sur.
George Robertson. Married by Rev. Griffith Dickinson. p. 38

30 June 1800. Elisha THACKER and Judith Hall. Sur. Reubin
Thacker. John Hall consents for Judith. p. 30

27 February 1792. John THACKER and Elizabeth Murphy, dau. of
Thomas Murphy who consents. Sur. Peter Thacker. Married by
Rev. Richard Elliott. p. 16

21 November 1789. Peter THACKER and Jenny Bradley. Married
by Rev. Richard Elliott. p. 12

5 September 1798. Randolph THACKER and Nancy Allen (widow).
Sur. Reubin Thacker. Married by Rev. James Tompkins. p. 26

8 March 1797. Reubin THACKER and Nancy Allen. Sur. Alex.
M.S. Allen. Married by Rev. Richard Elliott. p. 24

15 August 1791. John THARP and Lizann Saunders, dau. of
William Sanders who consents. Sur. Matthew Meglesson. Married
by Rev. Matthew Bates. p. 14

25 December 1792. Otho THARP and Jane Collwell (Caldwell?).
Married by Rev. Lazarus Dodson. p. 16

20 May 1786. George THOMAS and Elizabeth Bidwell. Sur. John
Biscow. p. 8

17 December 1798. Henson THOMAS and Nelly Boaz, dau. of Agness
Boaz who consents. Sur. John Thomas. Married by Rev. James
Tompkins. p. 26

17 November 1794. Lewis THOMAS and Pheby Holloway. Sur.
Joseph Flippen. Married by Rev. Richard Elliott. p. 19

23 ---- 1795. William THOMAS and Anne Campbell, dau. of
Abraham Campbell who consents. Sur. Richard Elliott. Married
by Rev. Richard Elliott. p. 21

-- ---- 1796. William THOMAS and Tabitha Madding. Married
by Rev. George Dodson. p. 23

19 September 1803. David THOMPSON and Mary V. Waller. Sur.
William Waller. Married by Rev. Thomas Payne. p. 36

8 September 1790. Jennings THOMPSON and Elizabeth Street.
Sur. Pyant Easley. Married by Rev. Richard Elliott. p. 13

16 August 1790. John THOMPSON and Sarah Fears. Sur. James
Turley. John Thompson son of William Thompson. Married by
Rev. Richard Elliott. p. 13

10 December 1787. Samuel THOMPSON and Peggy Carter. Sur.
Jesse Carter. Married by Rev. James Hinton. p. 10

2 December 1784. Walter THOMPSON and Wilmoth Shields. Married
by Rev. David Barr. p. 6

24 March 1795. William THOMPSON and Selah Duncan, dau. of
John Duncan who consents. Sur. John Wright. p. 21

28 August 1777. John THORNTON and Suvannah Pace, dau. of W.
Pace who consents. Sur. Stephen Coleman. p. 2

1 December 1784. Presley THORNTON and Mary Growley. Married
by Rev. David Barr. p. 6

16 December 1796. Richard THORNTON and Sarah Perkins, dau. of
Mary Perkins who consents. Sur. Isaac Potter. Married by
Rev. Clement Nance. p. 23

4 September 1796. William THORNTON and Elizabeth Cahall.
Married by Rev. Clement Nance. p. 23

6 January 1795. Zachariah THORNTON and Mary Oakes. Sur.
George Reynolds. p. 21

17 October 1785. Benjamin THRASHER and Sarah White, dau.
of Thomas White who consents. Sur. Tach Prenet. Married by
Rev. Lazarus Dodson. p. 7

7 November 1796. John THURMAN and Nancy Thomas. Sur. Jonathan
Thomas. Married by Rev. Richard Elliott. p. 23

5 March 1797. Laban THURMAN and Molley Morris Bow, dau. of
Gemyme Bow (mother). Sur. Nathaniel Bow. Married by Rev.
James Kinney. p. 24

18 June 1790. Nathan THURMAN and Levicy Barber. Sur. Ambrose
Collier. Signs her own consent. Married by Rev. James Kinney.
Nathan Thurman, father of Nathan signs certificate. (I think
this is an error and the groom himself signed it). p. 13

27 October 1794. Robert THURMAN and Peggey Robins. Sur.
Isham Dalton. Margill Robins consents for Peggey. Married
by Rev. James Kinney. p. 19

18 July 1781. William THURMAN and Susannah Brown. Married by Rev. Lewis Shelton. p. 3

19 September 1780. Richard TODD and Mary Lankford, dau. of Ben Lanford who consents. Sur. Joseph Akin. p. 3

7 February 1774. William TODD and Jane Shelton, dau. of Crispen Shelton who consents. Sur. John Greggory. p. 1

16 April 1798. Stephen TOLER and Peggy Pullen, dau. of Thomas and Peggy Pullen who consent. Sur. Joseph Toler. p. 26

29 June 1795. Thomas TOLLER and Anne Richardson, dau. of William Richardson who consents. Sur. Joseph Dodson. Married by Rev. John Atkinson. p. 21

2 November 1782. Jasper TOMBLIN and Alsey Abott. Married by Rev. James Robinson. p. 4

8 November 1792. Daniel TOMPKINS and Lydia Coner. Married by Rev. Clement Nance. p. 16

21 October 1793. George Jacob TOSH and Catherine Steven. Sur. James Henson. Signs her own consent. Married by Rev. James Kinney. p. 18

26 December 1794. William TOWLER and Agness Towler. Sur. Thomas Shockley. Signs her own consent. p. 19

19 July 1790. Halcoatt TOWNES and Anne Coleman. Sur. Richard N. Venable. p. 13

6 April 1791. Frederick TRUMP and Rhoda Hardey. Married by Rev. Richard Elliott. p. 14

13 August 1784. Moses TUCK and Susannah Nash. Married by Rev. David Barr. p. 6

15 December 1788. Nelson TUCKER and Martha Clark. Sur. William Clark. p. 11

1 January 1782. Robert TUCKER and Martha Shelton. Sur. Joseph Akin. Signs her own consent. p. 4

27 November 1784. James TURNER and Jane Anderson, dau. of Richard Anderson who consents. Sur. Abednego Turner. p. 6

5 January 1802. Jesse TURNER and Fanny Holligan, dau. of William Holligan who consents. Sur. Tollison Shumate. Married by Rev. Clement Nance. p. 34

19 July 1802. John TURNER and Caty Lankford. Sur. Stephen Lankford. Signs her own consent as Kittey Lankford. p. 34

2 September 1787. Moshack TURNER and Salley Farmer, dau. of James Farmer who consents. Sur. Joseph Akin. p. 10

21 May 1796. Stookley TURNER and Judith Coleman, dau. of Stephen Coleman who consents. Sur. Daniel Coleman. Married by Rev. Samuel D. Brame. p. 23

20 July 1789. William TUNSTALL and Jane Webb. Sur. Thomas Tunstall. Signs her own consent. Married by Rev. William Damison. p. 12

-- August 1783. John TURLEY and Martha Turley. Married by Rev. Lazarus Dodson. p. 5

21 December 1790. Leonard TURLEY and Susannah Marlows. Sur. John Dyer. p. 13

1 April 1801. Nathan TURLEY and Polley Shaw. Married by Rev. Thomas Payne. Sur. Henry Polley. p. 32

5 January 1792. Thomas Grine TURLEY and Amey Keesee. Married by Rev. Richard Elliott. p. 16

7 March 1796. Thomas TURLEY and Mary Justice. Sur. Nathan Turley. Married by Rev. Richard Elliott. p. 23

23 December 1799. Thomas TURLEY and Agness Childress, dau. of Richard Childress who consents. Sur. Robert Childress. p. 27

24 January 1800. William TURLEY and Sally Turley. Sur. Spencer Turley. James Turley consents for Sally. Married by Rev. Thomas Payne. p. 30

18 August 1797. Zachariah TURLEY and Peggy Childress. Sur. Robert Childress. p. 24

18 September 1805. Silas TWEEDWELL and Elizabeth Wilson, dau. of Basil Wilson who consents. Sur. Reason B. White. Married by Rev. James Nelson. p. 40

8 September 1800. Samuel TYREE and Dolley Moore. Sur. James Moore. p. 30

29 August 1796. Wilson VADEN and Rebecca Giles. Sur. Robert Adams. p. 23

16 December 1805. Silvanus A. VADIN and Polley Chatten, dau. of John Chatten, Sr., who consents. Polley also signs the certificate. Sur. Ephriam Giles. Married by Rev. David Nowlin. p. 40

18 June 1795. David VANCE and Bettsey Kremmer. Sur. Daniel Witcher. Christian Kremmer consents for Bettsey. Married by Rev. Thomas Douglas who says <u>Betsy Creamer</u>. p. 21

3 October 1800. Jacob VANCE and Judith Young, dau. of William Young who consents. Sur. Peyton Young. Married by Rev. John Wyatt. p. 30

31 December 1794. Drewry VAUGHAN and Sally Johns, dau. of Joseph Johns who consents. Sur. Edward Nunnelee. Married by Rev. Richard Elliott. p. 19

7 January 1805. William B. VAUGHAN and Sarah Terry, dau. of Joseph Terry who consents. Sur. Jeremiah Terry. Married by Rev. Griffith Dickinson. p. 40

-- ---- 1795. Thomas VILETS and Betsy Lug. Married by Rev. Matthew Bates. p. 21

17 September 1779. Ezekial VINCENT and Elizabeth Cooley, dau. of Jacob Cooley who consents and is surety. p. 2

13 July 1790. Ezekiel VINCENT and Darkes (Dorcas) Warren. Sur. John Warren. p. 13

21 February 1791. Jesse VINCENT and Ellenor Harvey. Sur. Leonard Sparks. p. 14

28 February 1791. Jesse VINCENT and Nancy Thomas. Married by Rev. Richard Elliott. p. 14

19 June 1779. William VINCENT and Glasey Cooley, dau. of Javob Cooley who consents. Sur. Joseph Akin. p. 2

9 January 1785. Peyton WADE and Mary Tarrents. Married by Rev. David Barr. p. 8

9 December 1792. Samuel WAGGONER and Mary Perkins. Married by Rev. Clement Nance. p. 16

-- ---- 1785. Charles WALDEN and Elizabeth Walls. Married by Rev. Nathaniel Thurman. p. 8

24 July 1802. Henry WALDEN and Maryann Kezee. Sur. Jesse Kezee. p. 34

13 December 1804. Lewis WALDEN and Milley Hunt, dau. of William Hunt who consents. Sur. John Hunt. p. 38

14 December 1797. Adam WALKER and Nancey Barnett. Sur. Anthony Holloway. Married by Rev. Lazarus Dodson. p. 24

19 November 1785. Charles WALKER and Nancy Allen Brewer, dau. of James Brewer who consents. Sur. Joseph Akin. Married by Rev. David Barr. p. 8

21 September 1787. Jeremiah WALKER and Mary Malicoat, dau. of John Malicoat who consents. Sur. Thomas Dyer. Married by Rev. Thomas Douglas. p. 10

27 May 1800. John WALKER and Betsey Walker. Sur. Moses Kirby. p. 30

15 September 1800. John WALKER and Betsey Jones. Sur. David F. Patrick. John Jones, guardian of Betsey, consents. p. 30

18 February 1799. Samuel WALKER and Elizabeth Parrish. Sur. Peter Parish. p. 28

10 January 1803. Thomas WALKER and Lucey Bayless. Sur. Mitchell Bayless. John Bayless, Sr., consents for Lucey. p. 36

22 March 1805. Vincent WALKER and Elizabeth Dove. Married by Rev. Griffith Dickinson. p. 40

9 September 1785. William WALKER and Betty Ward, dau. of Jeremiah Ward who consents. Sur. Thomas Ward. Married by Rev. David Barr. p. 8

6 January 1787. Henry WALL and Susannah Walters. Sur. William Walters. Married by Rev. Lazarus Dodson. p. 10

-- ---- 1799. Benjamin WALLER and Katherine Luck. Married by Rev. John Jenkins. p. 28

21 October 1805. Cuthbut WALLER and Elizabeth Compton, dau. of Archibald Compton who consents. Sur. Thomas Compton. p. 40

2 February 1793. Jonas WALLER and Mary Madding. Sur. William Madding. Married by Rev. Richard Elliott. p. 18

26 December 1805. Robert WALLER and Judith Craddock. Sur. John Waller. Signs her own consent. p. 40

23 January 1788. Archer WALLERS and Elizabeth Richards, dau. of Gabriel Richards who consents. Sur. William Murray. p. 11

6 August 1788. Benjamin WALROND and Lucy Ellinton. Married by Rev. Lazarus Dodson. p. 11

6 June 1796. John WALROND and Jane Parmer. Sur. Spencer Adams. Signs her own consent. Married by Rev. Lazarus Dodson. p. 23

18 February 1801. Reubin WALROND and Nancey Palmer. Sur. Jesse Walrond. Signs her own consent. p. 32

91

14 September 1801. Abraham WALTERS and Polly Mann, dau. of Jesse Mann Who consents. Sur. Joel Mann. p. 32

18 March 1793. Archer WALTERS and Edy Slayton, dau. of Daniel Slayton who consents. Sur. William Slayton. p. 18

16 October 1798. Archer WALTERS and Catey Stamps, dau. of John Stamps who consents. Sur. William Walters. Married by Rev. John Atkinson. p. 26

27 August 1803. Jackson WALTERS and Polley West Herring, dau. of William Herring who consents. Sur. Thomas Walters. Married by Rev. John Atkinson. p. 36

28 March 1782. John WALTERS and Mary Madding. Married by Rev. Lazarus Dodson. p. 5

7 July 1799. John WALTERS and Rhoda Walters, dau. of John Walters. Sur. Ezra Walters. p. 28

8 August 1803. Laban WALTERS and Nancy Chaney, dau. of Ezekel Chaney who consents. Sur. Thomas Chaney. Married by Rev. Elias Dodson. p. 36

20 December 1790. Obediah WALTERS and Aby Magby. Sur. Robert Madding. Signs her own consent. Married by Rev. John Atkinson. p. 13

9 December 1805. Thomas WALTERS and Betsy Tanner, grand dau. of Matthew Tanner who consents. Sur. Edmund Holloway. Married by Rev. John Atkinson. p. 40

10 December 1804. William WALTERS and Elizabeth Ball, dau. of John Ball who consents. Sur. Carter Ball. p. 38

24 January 1800. William WALTON and Salley Tanner. Sur. Croxon Green. Signs her own consent. p. 30

21 July 1789. George WARD and Elizabeth McMillion. Sur. Absolom Riley. p. 12

28 February 1793. George WARD and Rebeccah Bleakley. Married by Rev. Richard Elliott. p. 18

9 November 1799. John WARD and Fanney Collins, dau. of William and Mary Collins who consent. Sur. Joseph Akin. p. 28

7 November 1803. John WARD and Betsey Nelson. Sur. John Nelson. Married by Rev. David Nowlin. p. 36

18 November 1805. John WARD and Tabitha H. Walden. Sur.
Charles Walden. Married by Rev. Griffith Dickinson. p. 40

1 March 1791. Thomas WARD and Milley Walden. Sur. Charles
Walden. Married by Rev. Thomas Douglas. p. 14

10 February 1785. William WARE and Susannah Harrison. Married
by Rev. Samuel Harris. p. 8

15 November 1784. Edward WARIENT and Becky Dabney. Married
by Rev. Thomas Sparks. p. 6

30 June 1793. William WARREN and Mary Fuller. Sur. Jacob
Aaron. Married by Rev. Thomas Douglas. p. 18

23 January 1790. Joshua WASHBURN and Niley Dear, dau. of
Elizabeth Dear who consents. Sur. William Hankins. p. 13

22 October 1798. James WATKINS and Catey Burgess, dau. of
Jane Burgess who consents. Sur. John Burgess. p. 26

15 December 1794. Micajah WATKINS and Sarah Williams. Sur.
James A. Glenn. Married by Rev. John Atkinson. p. 19

20 November 1804. Abishal WATSON and Sally Watson. Sur.
William Watson, Jr. Married by Rev. Richard Elliott. p. 38

14 November 1793. Amos WATSON and Elizabeth Yats. Sur. Thomas
Watson. Stephen Yats consents for Elizabeth. Married by
Rev. Richard Elliott. p. 18

6 January 1791. Anderson WATSON and Sarah Streetman, dau.
of Elizabeth Streetman who consents. Sur. James Janscott. p. 14

20 October 1790. George WATSON and Peggy Murphy. Married by
Rev. Richard Elliott. p. 13

-- ---- 1793. Jacob WATSON and Mary Swenson. Sur. Joseph
Akin. p. 18

24 October 1782. John WATSON and Lurana Polley. Married by
Rev. John Bailey. p. 5

12 November 1784. John WATSON and Bethmiah Watson. Sur.
Will Watson. Married by Rev. Thomas Sparks. p. 6

22 November 1800. John WATSON, Jr., and Lucy Smith, dau. of
George Smith who consents. Sur. Thomas Watson, Jr. p. 30

16 November 1799. Joshua WATSON and Nancey Morray, dau. of
Elizabeth Morray who consents. Sur. John Bennett. p. 28

18 October 1798. Levi WATSON and Nancy Watson. Married by Rev. James Tompkins. p. 26

17 October 1792. Shemie WATSON and Elizabeth Murphy. Married by Rev. Richard Elliott. p. 16

21 November 1791. Thomas WATSON and Frances Campbell. Sur. William Watson. Married by Rev. Richard Elliott. p. 14

15 September 1800. Thomas WATSON and Melinda Watson, dau. of John Watson who consents and is surety. p. 30

12 January 1803. Berry WATTS and Bettsey Law, dau. of Mary Law who consents. Sur. Richard Ramsey. p. 36

3 December 1794. Joshua WATTS and Sarah Wright. Sur. Abednigo Harp. p. 19

19 August 1805. Levi WATTS and Betsey Ragsdale. Sur. Thomas Elliott. p. 40

30 March 1790. Money WEATHERFORD and Frances Spragens, dau. of William Spragens who consents. Sur. Joseph Akin. Married by Rev. Richard Elliott. p. 13

26 March 1778. John WEIR and Salley Burton, dau. of Charles Burton who consents. Sur. James Akin. p. 2

12 February 1797. Jonathan WELDON and Sarah Mayes. Sur. Gardner Mays. Married by Rev. John Atkinson. p. 24

19 November 1805. John WELLS and Fanney Seay. Sur. John Bullington. Both parties sign their own consent. Married by Rev. William Blair. p. 40

10 April 1794. Littleberry WELLS and Fanny Moodey. Married by Rev. James Kinney. p. 19

24 August 1803. James WEST and Nanny Crews, dau. of Jesse Crews who consents and is surety. p. 36

16 February 1789. John WEST and Mary West King. Sur. Benjamin Cannafas. Married by Rev. James Kinney. p. 12

25 October 1787. Richardson WHITBY and Sarah Hatfield. Married by Rev. Samuel Harris. p. 10

7 October 1778. Daniel WHITE and Molley Wade. Sur. John White. Signs her own consent. p. 2

4 August 1791.   Jeremiah WHITE and Lettice Shelton.   Married by Rev. John Bailey.   p. 14

14 February 1800.   Reason B. WHITE and Sally Nelson.   Sur. Robert Wright.   Married by Rev. Elias Dodson.   p. 30

8 February 1768.   Richard WHITE and Pegey (Peggy) Donald.   Sur. John Rowland.   p. 1

10 February 1767.   Richard WHITE and Margaret Donald.   Sur. John Cox.   p. 1

13 January 1795.   William WHITE and Nancy Shelton, dau. of John Shelton who consents.   Sur. Abraham Shelton.   Married by Rev. Thomas Payne.   p. 21

7 January 1804.   James WHITEHEAD and Elizabeth Markham, dau. of Mary Markham who consents.   Sur. Peter Markham.   Married by Rev. David Nowlin.   p. 38

1 March 1800.   William WHITEHURST and Mary Tanner, dau. of Matthew Tanner, Jr., who consents.   Sur. Daniel Everett.   p. 30

25 July 1778.   John WHITMELL and Catherine Asron.   Sur. Noton Dickinson.   Signs her own consent.   p. 2

19 July 1784.   William WHITTEN and Nelley Whitten.   Sur. William Burdett.   p. 6

30 July 1779.   William WILKINSON and Salley Dix.   Sur. John Dix.   p. 2

22 August 1803.   Abraham WILLIAMS and Salley Williams.   Sur. Abraham Williams, Sr.   Married by Rev. Clement Nance.   p. 36

3 March 1770.   Charles WILLIAMS and Ann Wilson.   Sur. Peter Wilson.   Signs her own consent.   p. 1

21 April 1783.   Charles WILLIAMS and Sarah Dix.   Sur. Peter Wilson.   Consent of James Dix for Sarah.   p. 5

26 January 1792.   David C. WILLIAMS and Lucy Terry, dau. of David Terry who consents.   Sur. James M. Williams.   Married by Rev. Lazarus Dodson.   p. 16

17 February 1794.   Doctor C. WILLIAMS and Nancy Wisdom, grand dau. of Francis Wisdom who consents.   Sur. Williams Williams. Married by Rev. Lazarus Dodson.   p. 19

15 November 1784.   James M. WILLIAMS and Wilmoth Walker. Sur. William White and John Crobin.   p. 6

16 July 1792. John WILLIAMS and Elizabeth Williams. Sur.
William Tunstall, Jr. R. Williams father (of which one?).
Married by Rev. Lazarus Dodson. p. 16

15 December 1798. John WILLIAMS and Betsey Gray, dau. of
Jeremiah Gray who consents. Sur. Joshua Gray. Married by
Rev. Clement Nance. p. 26

23 August 1803. John WILLIAMS and Tabitha Hardey. Sur.
Bannister Hardy. Married by Rev. Griffith Dickinson. p. 36

21 November 1792. Peter WILLIAMS and Salley Hill, dau. of
Isaac Hill who consents. Abner Parrott guardian of Peter.
Sur. Edwin Hammonds. p. 16

24 May 1787. Thomas T. WILLIAMS and Tabitha Walker. Consent
of Stephen Coleman (for which one?). Sur. James M. Williams.
Married by Rev. Lazarus Dodson. p. 10

2 July 1784. William WILLIAMS and Mary Lewis, dau. of John
Lewis who consents. Sur. Robert Lewis. p. 6

11 July 1789. William M. WILLIAMS and Elizabeth Adams, dau.
of John Adams who consents. Sur. Cain Adams. p. 12

4 March 1798. William WILLIAMS and Sarah Chattin, dau. of
John Chattin who consents and is surety. p. 26

14 April 1804. William WILLIAMS and Elizabeth May. Sur.
James May. Married by Rev. Thomas Sparks. p. 38

14 November 1803. James WILLIS and Martha Hoskins, dau. of
Thomas Hoskins who consents. Sur. William Hoskins. Married
by Rev. Thomas Payne. p. 36

2 November 1790. Joel WILLIS and Frances Meadows. Sur. Joab
Meadows. Married by Rev. John Atkinson. p. 13

10 December 1793. John WILLIS and Anne Payne. Sur. Giles
Payne. Married by Rev. Matthew Bates. p. 18

9 September 1797. Robert WILLIS and Elizabeth Blades. Sur.
William Bradley. Signs her own consent. p. 24

3 April 1779. Sterling WILLIS and Sarah Payne, dau. of
William Payne who consents. Sur. Joseph Akin. p. 2

18 August 1789. Thomas WILLIS and Molly Yates. Sur. Spencer
Shelton. p. 12

11 March 1803. William WILLIS and Polley Dalton. Sur.
William Haymes. Signs her own consent. Married by Rev. Thomas
Payne. p. 36

7 November 1801. Abel WILSON and Rhoda Creel. Sur. Elijah Creel. p. 32

26 January 1785. Charles WILSON and Caty Martin. Married by Rev. Lazarus Dodson. p. 8

11 July 1796. George WILSON, Jr., and Isabell Cunningham. Sur. Ephraim Cunningham. p. 23

15 June 1793. James WILSON and Mary Lynch. Married by Rev. Lazarus Dodson. p. 18

18 March 1793. John WILSON, Jr., and Sarah Lynch. Sur. Joseph Lynch. p. 18

15 December 1800. Martin WILSON and Rhoda Harris, dau. of John Harris who consents. Sur. Thomas Wilson. p. 30

-- ---- 1800. Martin WILSON and Rhoda Stamps. Married by Rev. Richard Elliott. p. 30

22 June 1780. William WILSON and Mary Dix, dau. of James Dix who consents. Sur. Hezekiah Smith. p. 3

11 March 1800. William WILSON and Jenny Thornton, dau. of Presley Thornton who consents. Sur. Moses Thornton. Married by Rev. Clement Nance. p. 30

10 December 1799. Caleb WITCHER and Giddy Watson. Sur. James Witcher. p. 28

22 December 1785. Daniel WITCHER and Salley Ward. Sur. Thomas Ward. Married by Rev. David Barr. p. 8

11 February 1796. Ephram WITCHER and Jensey Adams Rowden, dau. of Salley Rowden who consents. Sur. Tandy Witcher. p. 23

-- ---- 1800. Ephraim WITCHER and Jensey Adams. Married by Rev. Thomas Douglas. p. 30

1 November 1781. James WITCHER and Mary Colley. Married by Rev. Lewis Shelton. p. 3

-- ---- 1800. James WITCHER and Massey Watson. Married by Rev. Thomas Douglas. p. 30

1 April 1782. William WITCHER and Molley Dalton. Married by Rev. John Bailey. p. 5

28 September 1795. Nathaniel WOLSEY and Salley Keezee. Sur. John Keezee. p. 21

15 September 1800. Byrd WOMACK and Rebecca Haskins. Sur. John Haskins. Stephen Neal signs the certificate. p. 30

22 May 1797. Charles WOMACK, Jr., and Sally W. McDaniel, dau. of Clement McDaniel who consents. Sur. Byrd Womack. p. 24

4 January 1800. Drury WOODSON and Nanny Adams. Sur. William Williams. Cain Adams consents for Nancy. p. 30

-- ---- 1795. Tucker WOODSON and Anne Stolle. Married by Rev. Matthew Bates. p. 21

11 January 1786. Aaron WORLEY and Pattsey Bray, dau. of William Bray who consents. Sur. Hamon Dyer. Married by Rev. David Barr. p. 9

26 September 1792. Daniel WORSHAM and Elizabeth Gunnell. Sur. Robert Ferguson. Married by Rev. Lazarus Dodson. p. 16

-- ---- 1799. Francis WORSHAM and Molley Campbell. Married by Rev. Richard Elliott. p. 28

10 March 1782. Jeremiah WORSHAM and Ann McDowell. Married by Rev. John Bailey. p. 5

8 July 1785. John WORSHAM and Mourning Bennett. Married by Rev. David Barr. p. 8

-- March 1801. John WORSHAM, Jr., and Patsy Worsham. Sur. Jerry Shutt. John Worsham, Sr., guardian of Patsy, consents. p. 32

16 October 1797. Putram WORSHAM and Lucy Campbell. Sur. Jesse Richards. p. 24

16 July 1792. Charles WRIGHT and Rachel Doss, dau. of James Doss, Sr., who consents and is surety. p. 16

13 December 1803. Daniel WRIGHT and Sally Watts. Sur. John Wright. Married by Rev. Thomas Sparks. p. 36

14 April 1785. George WRIGHT and Sarah Vaden. Married by Rev. Lazarus Dodson. p. 8

28 June 1781. John WRIGHT and Avey Hardin. Married by Rev. John Bailey. p. 3

14 June 1785. John WRIGHT and Catharine Cook. Married by Rev. David Barr. p. 8

3 December 1794. John WRIGHT and Catherine Watts. Sur. Richard Watts. p. 19

20 December 1805. John WRIGHT and Polley Smith. Sur. Jesse Smith. Married by Rev. Richard Elliott. p. 40

12 April 1789. Joseph WRIGHT and Mary Adams, dau. of Alen Adams who consents. Sur. William Corbin. p. 12

4 March 1801. Richard P. WRIGHT and Esther Evans. Sur. Robert Evans. Married by Rev. Richard Elliott. p. 32

31 March 1786. Stith WYNNE and Phoebe Worsham. Sur. Daniel Worsham. p. 9

10 January 1793. James YANCEY and Nelley Bayne. Sur. William Glascock. Richard Bayne consents for Nelley. Married by Rev. Hawkins Landrum. p. 18

17 March 1795. Samuel YATES and Polley Davis. Married by Rev. Thomas Payne. p. 21

20 December 1803. Joseph YEATES and Betsy Johnson. Sur. James Johnson. Signs her own consent. Married by Rev. John Jenkins. p. 36

15 October 1799. Stephen YEATES, Jr., and Polley Hall. Sur. Amos Watson. Married by Rev. Richard Elliott. p. 28

19 June 1804. Joseph YEATTS and Salley Linthicum, dau. of Thomas Linthicum who consents and is surety. Married by Rev. Richard Elliott. p. 38

16 December 1799. Tarpley YEATTS and Dianna Dodson. Sur. Fortunand Dodson. p. 28

12 February 1785. George YOUNG, Jr., and Nancy Hampton. Sur. Jesse Hodges. Married by Rev. David Barr. p. 8

17 October 1795. Joshiah YOUNG and Elizabeth Ferrell. Sur. Joseph Dotson. p. 21

1 May 1792. Marlin YOUNG and Tabitha Witcher, dau. of Daniel Witcher who consents. Sur. John Weatherford. Married by Rev. Thomas Douglas. p. 16

13 September 1790. Melton YOUNG and Nancy Witcher, dau. of Daniel Witcher who consents. Sur. Peyton Young. Married by Rev. Thomas Douglas who says Milton Young. p. 13

27 February 1795. Peyton YOUNG and Elizabeth Oglesby. Sur. Field Allen Duncan. Married by Rev. Thomas Douglas. p. 21

22 May 1804. Samuel YOUNG and Peggy Vance. Sur. David Vance. Married by Rev. Joseph Hatchett. p. 38

****

Bolton		
Elizabeth	67	
Mildred	51	
Booker		
Rebecca	27	
Bow		
Molley Morris	87	
Boyd		
Elley	80	
Bradley		
Jenny	86	
Nancy	37	
Polley	62	
Sarah	56	
Branner		
Mirrah	61	
Branson		
Rebecca	68	
Brawner		
Mary	27	
Nancy	73	
Bray		
Pattsey	98	
Brevins		
Barbary	81	
Brewer		
Nancy Allen	91	
Pattsey	11	
Patty	72	
Brewis		
Polley	59	
Bridgewater		
Fanny	32	
Briscoe		
Charity	70	
Sally	50	
Brock		
Elizabeth	35	
Brogin		
Nancy	22	
Brooks		
Rachel	21	
Tabitha	1	
Browden		
Mary Aney	52	
Brown		
Anne	49	
Polley	16	
Rhodey	60	
Sally	69	
Sarah	44, 62	
Susanna	35,70, 88	
Bruce		
Caty	27	
Sally	75	
Bryant		
Elizabeth	43	
Bucey		
Casey	31	
Mille	44	

Buckley		
Elizabeth	41	
Bucknell		
Blanche	85	
Mary	84	
Bumpass		
Ann	19	
Burch		
Mary	78	
Bruges-Burgess		
Catey	93	
Elizabeth	14	
Jane	69	
Mary	16,39	
Nancy	45	
Sarah	12	
Susannah	11	
Virlena	81	
Burnett		
Alice	40	
Elizabeth	13,81	
Nancy	52	
Polley	67,71	
Burton		
Febe (Phoebe)	8	
Judith	18	
Nancy	1	
Salley	94	
Sarah	64	
Susanna	45	
Suvanna	28	
Butcher		
Lydia	66	
C		
Cabell		
Bethinia	65	
Cahall		
Bethania	66	
Elizabeth	87	
Cahill		
Abbe	58	
Caldwell		
Martha	43	
Callam		
Elizabeth	70	
Callands		
Anna B.	14	
Elizabeth	14	
Callaway		
Sally	3	
Cammeron		
Nancy	57	
Campbell		
Agness	1	
Anne	86	
Elizabeth	16	
Frances	94	
Jane	50	
Lucy	98	
Milley	49	
Molley	98	
Sally	70	

Carter		
Frances	43	
Mary	43	
Peggy	87	
Chambers		
Betsey	21	
Nancy	1	
Chaney-Chany		
Ann	42	
Elizabeth	52	
Nancy	92	
Polley	52	
Sally	12	
Vicey	57	
Chatmon		
Elizabeth	34	
Chatten-Chattin		
Frances	1	
Polley	89	
Sarah	96	
Cheatham		
Lucy	40	
Chick		
Lucy	60	
Childress		
Agnes	89	
Isabel	32	
Peggy	89	
Chilton		
Rachel	23	
Church		
Elizabeth	22	
Sally	68	
Clark-Clarke		
Archer	48	
Carolin M.	80	
Catharine	23	
Mary Polly	69	
Martha	88	
Pheby	11	
Clarkson		
Fanny	9	
Claybourne		
Susanna	19	
Cline		
Molly	16	
Clopton		
Betsy	69	
Fanny	85	
Molly	82	
Cockram		
Elizabeth	44	
Coe		
Mary	29	
Sarah	28	
Coleman		
Anne	76,88	
Elizabeth	59	
Judith	89	
Lucy	68	
Polley	18	
Sarah	72	
Colley		
Mary	97	

Collie
  Peggy   47

Collier
  Anne   2
  Mary   35

Colligan
  Maryann   30

Collins
  Fanny   92
  Nancy   50
  Polly   59

Collwell
  Jane   86

Combs
  Mary   33

Compton
  Anne   71
  Elizabeth   91
  Lena   4
  Polley   22

Coner
  Lydia   88

Conn
  Elizabeth   36

Conneley
  Elizabeth   36

Conner
  Sarah   6

Conway
  Lucy   39
  Mary   10

Cook
  Catharine   98
  Elizabeth   29
  Frances   10
  Nancy   73
  Priscilla   29
  Sarah   22

Cooley
  Elizabeth   59,90
  Gleasey   90
  Nancy   70
  Sally Jordan   72

Cooper
  Pattsey   84

Corbin
  Anne   55
  Delah Ann   32
  Milley   49
  Sarah   2
  Susanna   61

Cornwell
  Elizabeth   17

Cottrell
  Molley   34

Covington
  Betsy   38
  Susanna   54

Cox
  Charity   61
  Prudence   58

Craddock
  Judith   91
  Priscilla   60
  Sarah   60

Crain-Crane
  Elizabeth   52
  Frankey   16
  Jobil   79
  Nancy   22
  Sally   39

Crawford
  Elizabeth   17

Creamer
  Betsy   90

Creek
  Rhoda   97

Crenshaw
  Sarah   29

Crews
  Nanny   94

Crider
  Caty   23

Cross
  Lucretia   75

Crus
  Elizabeth   65

Crust
  Barbery   2

Crutchfield
  Jincey   85

Culley
  Pheba   20

Cundiff
  Levincy   54
  Lucy   54

Cunningham
  Elizabeth   21
  Isabell   97
  Jane   66,72
  Lucy   17
  Martha   36
  Mary   79
  Nancy   17
  Polley   33
  Sarah   8

Curry
  Barbary   15

D

Dabney
  Becky   93

Daine
  Elizabeth   62

Dalton
  Agitha   56
  Ann   38
  Asenna   8
  Betsy   43
  Edythe   55
  Jean   41
  Jenny   38
  Judith   66
  Mary   44

Dalton (cont'd)
  Mioly   80
  Molley   23,97
  Nancy   8,28,86
  Polley   96
  Sally   66
  Sarah   38

Daniel
  Frances   11
  Keziah   38

Davis
  Anne   58
  Catherine   15
  Elizabeth   10,17
  Frances   74
  Lucy   9, 43
  Margaret   15
  Mary   37
  Milley   46
  Nancy   3, 71
  Polley   99
  Sarah   55
  Seludy   74
  Susanna   (2)19

Dawson
  Ann J.   6
  Polley   31

Deacon
  Peggy Arch   78

Dean
  Margaret   22

Dear
  Alincy   4
  Niley   93

Debo
  Betsy   73
  Christina   21

Dejarnet
  Eda   75

Delosiea
  Jaenea   17

Denton
  Nancy   44,46
  Peggy   60
  Polley   24

Depea
  Elizabeth   58

Deropit
  Nancy   12

Devin
  Margaret   70

Dickinson
  Polley   8

Dix
  Betsey   52
  Fanney   64
  Henrietta   2
  Martha   65
  Mary   97
  Patsey   42
  Salley   95
  Sarah   95

Dixon
  Betsy   57
  Mary   33

Dodson
- Dianna 99
- Dicey 15
- Elizabeth 15
- Fanny 32
- Ludy 26
- Lyda 68
- Margaret 20
- Mary 53
- Milley 72
- Miriam 71
- Nancy 70
- Nelly 32
- Patsey 14
- Rosannah 7
- Sarah 32, 74
- Tabitha 26, 66
- Unity 26

Donald
- Margaret 95
- Pegey (Peggy) 95

Donelson
- Sally 55

Doss
- Anne 55
- Elizabeth 3
- Judah 29
- Lucy 12
- Rachel 98

Douglas
- Edith 12
- Locky 59

Dove
- Amily 37
- Ann 74
- Elizabeth 91
- Polley 72
- Winifred 4

Dudley
- Mary 52
- Sarah 73
- Susannah 74

Duncan
- Selah 87

Dunn
- Bucy 54
- Crusey 68
- Mary 12

Dupea-Dupey
- Sarah 74
- Susanna 74

Durat
- Leah 40

Durham
- Elizabeth 38

Durret
- Patsey 50

Dyer
- Agness 23
- Amey 7, 11
- Annice 13
- Elender 5
- Nany 2
- Peggy 41
- Polley 35
- Winney 4

E

Earls
- Judith 55
- Nancy 27

Early
- Polley 57

Earp
- Drucilla 16
- Sarah 51

Easley
- Nancy 34

Echols
- Betsey 31
- Frances E. 78

Ellington
- Lucy 91
- Nancy 47
- Obedience 51
- Sarah 28

Elliott
- Belinda 79
- Betsey 68
- Elizabeth 35
- Mary 68
- Nancy 50
- Salley 36, 65
- Susanna 14, 51, 79

Emmerson
- Elizabeth 30
- Rachel 4

Epperson
- Martha 24
- Nancy 9

Evans
- Esther 99

Everet-Everett
- Catharine 31
- Peggey 19

F

Falling
- Ruth 37

Fallon
- Rebeckah 36

Farmer
- Anne 46
- Elizabeth 77, 84
- Jensey 67
- Mary 29
- Salley 1, 29, 89

Faris-Farris
- Eunice 73
- Jane 71
- Keziah 32
- Nancy 64

Farthing
- Beckey 64
- Marshall 62

Fearn-Fearns
- Elizabeth Lee 65
- Joice 45
- Leannah 64
- Lucy 65

Fears
- Sarah 87

Ferguson
- Elizabeth 8
- Millicent 36
- Nancy 54
- Polley 12
- Priscilla 17
- Rhodey 52
- Stony 7
- Susannah 36

Ferrell
- Elizabeth 99

Fielder
- Nancy 47

Fitzgerald
- Abbygie (Abigail) 83
- Elizabeth 83
- Frances 25, 27
- Lightee 39
- Susanna 43

Flippin
- Elizabeth 76
- Patsey 42

Flowers
- Jane 17
- Milly 50

Fontaine
- Elizabeth 7

Ford
- Elizabeth 85
- Nancy 70
- Polly 37
- Rebecca 16

Formby
- Polley 24

Foster
- Clara 46
- Winifred 23

Fouster
- Zuriah 39

Fowlkes
- Editha 81
- Salley 43

Fuller
- Elizabeth 3
- Mary 93
- Polley 44
- Rachel 50

Fulton
- Martha 8

Furbush
- Nancy 74

G

Gallilee
- Charlotte 23

Gammon
- Agness 61

Gannaway
- Polley 36

Garner
Elizabeth 77
Polly 53

George
Mary 41, 72

Gibson
Jaibey 40

Gilbert
Elizabeth 75
Levency 42
Mary 35
Sarah 21

Giles
Patty 79
Rebecca 89

Glasco-Glascoe
Elizabeth 67
Nelly 67

Glenn
Patsy 46

Goad
Jean 5
Mary 23
Nancy 5

Goard
Elizabeth 17

Going
Jenny 8

Gooch
Ann 10

Goodman
Susanna 25

Gord
Elizabeth 37

Gorman
Diadamy 41

Gosnell
Nancy 6

Goven
Ruth 36

Gover
Elizabeth 68
Margaret 34
Nancy 18

Gowing
Sythe 15

Gray
Any 24
Betsey 96
Elizabeth 39

Gravelly
Polly 60

Griffey
Betsey 49

Griggory
Maryan P. 65

Grisham
Nancy 22, 70
Rhoda 22

Groff
Catey 21
Tinah 53

Growley
Mary 87

Grubbs
Susanna 61

Gunnell
Elizabeth 78
Frances 32

Guthrey
Elizabeth 46

Gwin
Elizabeth 31

H

Hackworth
Seany 39

Hains
Patsey 21

Haley
Joannah 59

Hall
Elizabeth 92
Frances 11
Judith 86
Margaret 75
Mary 41
Polley 99
Salley 40
Susannah 75

Hamblin
Susanna 37

Hamlet
Rachel 63

Hammock
Mary 10,80

Hampton
Elenor 41
Margaret 19
Nancy 99

Hands
Elizabeth 61
Mary 61

Hankins
Elizabeth I. 19
Jane 19
Peggy 22
Rebecca 4

Hannah
Polley 60

Hanoon
Dorcas 70

Hardey-Hardy
Frances 7
Nancy 51
Polley 51
Rhoda 88
Sarah 50
Tabitha 96

Hardin
Avey 98

Haring
Jensy 48

Harnes-Harness
Betsy 6
Elizabeth 54
Martha 35

Harp
Christina 75

Harris
Elizabeth 66
Jane 12
Keziah 39
Lucey 67
Nancy 5
Peggy 18
Polly 12,59
Rhoda 97

Harrison
Anna Payne 18
Chaney 57
Elizabeth 74
Jane Payne 83
Marriam 83
Patsy 32
Sarah 37
Susanna 83,93

Harvey
Ellener 90
Linda 13

Haskins
Rebecca 98

Hatfield
Sarah 94

Hawker
Elizabeth 75
Lydea 70

Hayes
Dianna 46

Hayne
Elizabeth 79

Headrick-Hedrick
Peachy 69
Peggy 5

Henderson
Ann 71

Hendrick
Elizabeth 80
Mary 19
Patsey 27
Tabitha (2)26

Henry
Anna 68

Hensley
Lucy 62

Henson
Elizabeth 66
Alce B. 66

Herring
Ermin 31
Polley West 92

Hester
Polley 9

Hill
- Lurane 38
- Mary 9
- Salley 96
- Susannah 15

Hillard
- Elizabeth 47

Hinson
- Lettice 47

Hodges
- Dorceas 63
- Elizabeth 44
- Mary 48

Hodnett
- Jane 24
- Lucy 24
- Nancy 24
- Sarah 85

Holder
- Elizabeth 27
- Milley 43
- Molley 43, 66

Hollagan-Holligan
- Fanny 88
- Jenny 72
- Judith 71

Holloway
- Christa 15
- Frances 18
- Jane 32
- Pheby 86

Holton
- Charlotte 72

Hopkins
- Fanny 11

Hopper
- Betsy 60

Hopson
- Mildred 22

Horner
- Rhodey 33

Hoskins
- Martha 96

Hoyle
- Mary 11

Hubbard
- Betsy 31
- Edy 83
- Elizabeth 42
- Molley 54
- Nancy 58
- Sarah Waren 56

Hudson
- Amy 84
- Nancy 58
- Polley 25
- Sally 72

Hudspeth
- Nancy 43

Huffman
- Catharine 71
- Nancy 43

Humphrey
- Barsha 81
- Caty 46

Hundley
- Arabella 26
- Polley 11

Hunt
- Milley 90

Hurt
- Jane 41
- Nancy 78
- Rhoda 77

Hutcherson
- Nancy 39

Hutchings
- Elizabeth 63
- Mildred 61

Hutison
- Nancy 20

I

Ingram
- Leety 55
- Patsy 29

Inman
- Lydia 9
- Nancy 57

Irby
- Jane 78
- Nancy 84
- Rebecca 53

Ivey
- Betsy 71

J

Jaetz
- Susanna 54

James
- Frankey 9
- Nancy 37

Jefferson
- Frances 58

Jeffress-Jeffreys
- Patsy 22

Jenkins
- Elizabeth 38
- Jane S. 57
- Mary 31
- Nancy 24

Jennings
- Agness 59
- Elizabeth 43
- Nancy 18

Johns
- Gartherhood 50
- Sally 90

Johnson
- Betsy 99
- Elizabeth C. 78
- Ginsey 65
- Nancy 68
- Rebecca 44
- Salley 62

Jolley
- Charity 46
- Sarah 63

Jones
- Ann 24
- Betsey 91
- Mary B. 6
- Mary 45
- Nancy 24
- Polley 47

Justice
- Elizabeth 67
- Mary 89
- Polley 80
- Sarah 64

K

Kearby
- Judith 3

Keatts
- Elizabeth 12
- Martha 77
- Mary 17

Keen
- Christian 34

Kendrick
- Massy 27

Keesee, Kezee, Keezee
- Amey 36,89
- Anny 66
- Elizabeth 42
- Jincy 85
- Mary 23
- Maryan 90
- Nancy 10
- Pinnah 53
- Polley 21
- Sally 97
- Susanna 2
- Tabitha 54

Kerby-Kirby
- Elenor 49
- Judith 3
- Martha 28
- Sarah 20,63

Kimens
- Jane 79

King
- Mary West 94
- Nancy 85
- Polley 26

Kremmer
- Bettsey 90

L

Lamb
- Fanny 48

Lambeth
- Sarah 69

Lancaster
- Betsey 33

Lane
- Judith 32

Laneford
- Smithey 40

Morris
    Anna   25

Morton
    Cecelia M.   57
    Elizabeth V.   60
    Jane   3
    Viney   28

Morray
    Nancey   93

Morrice
    Hannah   83

Motley-Mottley
    Amy   14
    Delilah   85
    Elizabeth   34
    Prudence   83
    Salley   2

Muckmillion
    Nelley   71

Mullings-Mullins
    Anna   63
    Nelly   37
    Patty   6
    Sally   29

Murphy
    Elizabeth   86, 94
    Jaley   36
    Peggy   93

Murray-Murry
    Cloe   40
    Elizabeth   12
    Saphira   75

Muse
    Elizabeth   84
    Fanny Chatten   84
    Janey   38

Musteen-Mustain
    Anne   5
    Luedy   76
    Polley   64
    Priscilla   78
    Salley   79
    Susanna   35

Myers
    Salley   38

N

Nance
    Dorothy   13
    Susanna   76

Nash
    Anne   76
    Frances   82
    Lettice   85
    Mary   28, 53
    Susanna   88

Neal
    Ann   (2) 48
    Lucy   83
    Sally   85

Nelson
    Betsey   92
    Lucy   76
    Peggy   63
    Rhoda   76
    Sally   95

Newbil
    Betsey   20

Norton
    Anne   24
    Elizabeth   69
    Jane   10
    Martha   84

Nowlin-Nowling
    Caty   8
    Elizabeth   25
    Lucy   8
    Lukey   25
    Mary   53
    Susanna   25

Nuckols
    Rozanna   22

O

Oaks-Oakes
    Elizabeth   71
    Janes   75
    Mary   87
    Nancy   27
    Salley   67

Odanial-O'Daniel
    Nancy   69
    Peggy   59

Oglesby
    Elizabeth   99

Ogletree
    Nancy   37

Oliver
    Elizabeth   4
    Frances   50
    Martha   21
    Mary   21

Oneal
    Barbary   75
    Peggy   81

Owen-Owin
    Agness   66
    Jean   59
    Lidia   2
    Lucy   50
    Nancy   82
    Patsey   18
    Sally   2, 6

P

Pace
    Suvannah   87

Pain-Paine
    Agness   40
    Caty   63

Palmer
    Nancy   91

Parham
    Archer   83

Parks
    -----   45
    Martha   45
    Mary   63

Parker
    Frankey   63

Parker (cont'd)
    Milley   20
    Nancy   20

Parmer (Palmer?)
    Jane   91

Parish-Parrish
    Elizabeth   91
    Nancy   25

Parrott
    Michal   39
    Oney   10

Parsons
    Betsey   48
    Lydia   56
    Mary   56
    Mishel   64
    Sarah   64

Patrick
    Ann   11
    Elizabeth F.   57

Patterson
    Agatha   23
    Elizabeth   23
    Nancy   4

Payne
    Abigail   3
    Anne   40,77,96
    Deborah   42
    Fanny   78
    Janey   1
    Ketturah   27
    Lucresia   66
    Mary   28,45
    Sally   22,82
    Sarah   6
    Susannah   47

Pears
    Nancy   55

Pearson
    Chloe   1
    Milley   72
    Sarah   17

Pemberton
    Joicey   29
    Sarah   16

Pendleman
    Elizabeth   57
    Sarah   6

Perdue
    Nelly   3

Perkins
    Anna   56
    Bethania   81
    Betsey   25
    Dorchas   48
    Elizabeth 50,69
    Jane   17
    Mary   90
    Patsey   56
    Sarah   87

Petty
    Elizabeth   12

Phillips
    Hannah   42
    Milley   25
    Polley   49
    Susanna   82

Picknall
    Luvania   23

Pigg
    Anne   28
    Betsey   72
    Edey   63
    Martha   80
    Rachel   7

Pistole
    Winifred   49

Polley
    Lurana   93
    Lydia   84
    Sally   30

Porter
    Susanna   55

Potter
    Jeriah   48

Powel-Powell
    Keziah   39
    Mary   55
    Nancy   84
    Patsey   55

Prewet-Prewett
    Aggy   37
    Elizabeth   13
    Polley   41
    Rossey   47
    Susanna   62
    Wealthy   4

Price
    Anne   20
    Dice   59
    Hannah   73
    Joyce   82
    Molley   59
    Nancy   83
    Pattsy   59
    Polley   84
    Susanna   2

Prosize
    Martha   62
    Sally   10, 36

Pruet-Pruett
    Elizabeth   67
    Frances   19
    Rachel   51

Pryor
    Elizabeth   83

Pulliam
    Keziah   13
    Nancy   71
    Peechie   61

Pullen-Pullin
    Patsey   7
    Peggy   88
    Sarah   23

Purnell
    Mary   26

Q

Quinn
    Elizabeth   37

R

Ragland
    Nancy   20
    Salley   54

Ragsdale
    Betsey   94
    Polley   30

Ramsey
    Anna   47
    Levina   46
    Nancy   46
    Polley   3
    Susannah   18

Razon
    Margaret   33

Read
    Mary H.   40
    Peggy   51

Reice
    Sarah   12

Reiger
    Betsy   34
    Rozanna   15
    Sally   34

Reiter
    Molley   41

Reither
    Mary   36

Reynolds
    Anna Davis   41
    Bettsey   44
    Judith   54
    Lucy   67
    Nancy   11
    Patsey   5
    Susanna   44

Richards
    Anney   30
    Elizabeth   73,91
    Milley   65,79
    Rachel   19

Richardson
    Anne   88
    Mary   40
    Sarah   27,61
    Susanna   56

Ridel
    Sarah   34

Rider
    Yuleanna   20

Right
    Elizabeth   39

Rigney
    Drucilla   84
    Rebekah   56

Riter
    Mary   21

Roach
    Frances   31

Robbin
    Ellenor   6

Robins
    Peggey   87

Roberts
    Caty   19
    Elley   31
    Eugan   55
    Polley(alias Bingham)11
    Samoras   47
    Susanna   78
    Upham   55

Robertson
    Betsey   84
    Jane   33
    Molley   14
    Patsey   13
    Selah   86

Robinson
    Elenor   50
    Freelove   58
    Margaret   13
    Mary   47
    Polley   41

Rodd
    Elizabeth   81

Rogers
    ----   61
    Beckey   14
    Elizabeth   70
    Mary   10
    Susanna   79

Rollin
    Nancy   73

Ross
    Nancy   77

Rossett
    Elizabeth   2

Rowden
    Jensey Adams   97
    Tabitha   20

Rowland
    Phebe   74

Royall
    Polley   2

Russell
    Patsey   81
    Prudence   73
    Salley   9
    Wilmoth   14

Rutledge
    Ann   52

S

Samson
    Mary   28

Sanders-Saunders
    Catherine   24
    Dorcas   45
    Lizann   86
    Patty   21
    Ruth   6
    Susanna   55

Scott
    Anne   3

Wilkinson
    Elizabeth   50
    Salley   35

Williams
    Alice   2
    Constance   30
    Elizabeth   96
    Judith   30
    Lucinda   14
    Martha   41
    Mary   16
    Nancy   35, 42
    Nancy R.   48
    Polley   18
    Polly W.   45
    Rebeccah   46
    Salley   95
    Sarah (2) 33, 52, 93
    Sibbe   30
    Susanna   21, 78

Willis
    Avey   49
    Elizabeth   28
    Nancy   44
    Susannah   20

Wilson
    Ann   95
    Elizabeth   89
    Esebell   1
    Isabella   35
    Jane Cook   16
    Leah   82
    Margaret   4
    Mary   50
    Nelly   47
    Polly   16
    Rachel   65
    Sally   50

Wimbish
    Polly   49

Widsom
    Mary   20
    Nancy   95

Witcher
    Anna   51
    Elizabeth   70
    Nancy   99
    Rhoda   53
    Sally   69
    Tabitha   99

Witt
    Susanna   6

Womack
    Elizabeth   15

Wood
    Sally   66

Woodson
    Jean   10
    Judith   30
    Nancy   47
    Sarah   30

Worsham
    Elizabeth   29
    Patsy   98
    Patsy W.   83
    Phoebe   99
    Temperance   34

Wright
    Frances   76
    Margaret   32

Wright (cont'd)
    Martha   73
    Milley   19
    Patsey   82
    Salley   83
    Sarah   94
    Rosamond   31

Wynne
    Christian   9

Y

Yates
    Molly   96

Yats
    Elizabeth   93

Yeatts
    Salley   39

Young
    Elizabeth   48
    Judith   90